Comparative Discrimination Law

# Comparative Discrimination Law



Volumes published in this Brill Research Perspectives title are listed at *brill.com/rpcd*

# Comparative Discrimination Law

*Historical and Theoretical Frameworks*


*By*

Laura Carlson



BRILL

LEIDEN | BOSTON

This paperback book edition is simultaneously published as issue 1.1 (2017) of *Comparative Discrimination Law*, DOI 10.1163/24522031-12340001.

Library of Congress Control Number: 2017956215

Typeface for the Latin, Greek, and Cyrillic scripts: "Brill". See and download: brill.com/brill-typeface.

ISBN 978-90-04-34544-7 (paperback)
ISBN 978-90-04-34545-4 (e-book)


Published by Koninklijke Brill NV, Leiden, The Netherlands.
Koninklijke Brill NV incorporates the imprints Brill, Brill Hes & De Graaf, Brill Nijhoff, Brill Rodopi, Brill Sense and Hotei Publishing.


This book is printed on acid-free paper and produced in a sustainable manner.

# Contents

# Preface

This volume is the first in the Brill Research Perspectives series concerning comparative discrimination law. This series addresses comparative discrimination issues both horizontally (overarching frameworks) and vertically (specific issues within discrimination law). Topics include unlawful discrimination on the basis of race, sex, religion, age, disability, gender, sexual orientation, as well as intersectionality—at national, regional, and international levels. Theoretical as well as more pragmatic approaches, such as the use of active measures to combat structural discrimination and proving discrimination claims with empirical evidence, are also explored. Law by its nature is bound by culture and language, and the effort in the series has been made to examine issues of discrimination from different jurisdictions. The editors welcome suggestions as to authors and jurisdictions outside those presented in the volumes to date. This series is to run for ten years of quarterly volumes, with the ambition to achieve a broad approach to comparative discrimination law issues.

# Abbreviations

| | |
|---|---|
| ACAS | UK Advisory, Conciliation and Arbitration Services |
| AD | Swedish Labour Court |
| AU | African Union |
| CEDAW | UN Convention of the Elimination of All Forms of Discrimination against Women |
| CIS | Commonwealth of Independent States |
| CJ | European Union Court of Justice (Luxemburg) |
| CLS | Critical Legal Studies |
| CMW | UN International Convention on the Protection of the Rights of All Migrant Workers and Members of Their Families |
| COE | Council of Europe |
| CRC | UN Convention on the Rights of the Child |
| CRPD | UN Convention on the Rights of Person with Disabilities |
| CRT | Critical Race Theory |
| DO | Swedish Discrimination Ombudsman |
| DOL | US Department of Labor |
| EAT | UK Employment Appeal Tribunal |
| EC | European Community |
| ECHR | European Convention for the Protection of Human Rights and Fundamental Freedoms, aka European Convention |
| ECSC | The European Coal and Steel Community |
| ECtHR | European Court of Human Rights (Strasbourg) |
| EEC | European Economic Community |
| EEOC | US Equal Employment Opportunity Commission |
| EHRC | UK Equality and Human Rights Commission |
| EO | US Presidential Executive Order |
| EPA | US Equal Pay Act |
| EU | European Union |
| EU Charter | Charter on Fundamental Rights of the European Union |
| Euratom | The European Atomic Energy Community |
| Euro | Currency of the European Union |
| FEP | US Fair Employment Practices |
| FMLA | US Family and Medical Leave Act |
| GINA | Genetic Information Nondiscrimination Act of 2008 |
| IACHR | Inter-American Commission on Human Rights |
| ICCPR | UN International Covenant on Civil and Political Rights |

| | |
|---|---|
| ICERD | UN International Convention on the Elimination of All Forms of Racial Discrimination |
| ICESCR | UN International Covenant on Economic, Social and Cultural Rights |
| ILO | International Labour Organization |
| JämO | Swedish Equal Opportunity (Women and Men) Ombudsman |
| LGBTQIA | Lesbian, gay, bisexual, transgender, queer and questioning, intersex and intergender and anonymous and ally |
| LO | Swedish Landsorganisation |
| MHRA | Minnesota Human Rights Act |
| Minn.Stat. | Minnesota statute |
| NAACP | National Association for the Advancement of Colored Persons |
| NGO | Non-governmental Organization |
| OAS | Organization of American States |
| OAU | Organisation of African Unity |
| OFCCP | US Office of Federal Contract Compliance Programs |
| OIC | Organisation of Islamic Cooperation |
| SAF | The Swedish Employers Confederation (*Svenska arbetsgivareföreningen*) |
| SEK | Swedish crowns currency |
| TEU | Treaty of the European Union |
| TFEU | Treaty of the Functioning of the European Union |
| Title VII | Title VII of the US Civil Rights Act of 1964 |
| UK | The United Kingdom |
| UN | United Nations |
| UNDHR | United Nations Declaration of Human Rights |
| US | The United States |
| WHD | US Department of Labor, Wage and Hours Division |

# Comparative Discrimination Law: Historical and Theoretical Frameworks

*Laura Carlson*

## Introduction: Comparative Discrimination Law

Human history is marked by group and individual struggles for emancipation, equality and self-expression. This first volume in the Brill Research Perspectives in Comparative Discrimination Law briefly explores some of the history underlying these efforts in the field of discrimination law. A broad discussion of the historical development of issues of discrimination is first set out, looking at certain international, regional and national bases for modern discrimination legal structures. Several of the theoretical frameworks invoked in a comparative discrimination law analysis are then addressed, either as institutional frameworks or theories addressing specific protection grounds. The disclaimer must be made that this volume is dedicated to setting out an introduction to the field of comparative discrimination law, and consequently, cannot in any way be seen as covering the entire flora of issues and theories existing within this very compelling topic.

A brief discussion as to terminology is warranted. Language is essential when articulating the discrimination protections, rights and liberties to be granted to individuals and groups. Many prefer to discuss these issues in terms of equality, others anti-discrimination or non-discrimination, while others discrimination rights. The choice here has been to call this series Comparative Discrimination Law, much in the same way as we discuss criminal law or tort law, discrimination as the subject-matter of the field. However, this choice is simply pragmatic, and in no way meant to exclude issues of equality or non-discrimination. Other than the actual title of the series, the contributing authors freely choose their own terminology.

The historical treatment of discrimination issues on the international, then regional and certain national levels is first explored. The carving out of discrimination protections is intimately intertwined with recognizing civil rights, particularly legal personhood, citizenship and voting rights, labor and employment rights, and human rights. The abolition of the institution of slavery is one

 | DOI 10.1163/9789004345454_001

of the initial driving forces as to legal discrimination protections in modern Western legal systems, with the emancipations of workers and women following closely on its heels. The protected grounds of religion, age, disability, sexual orientation and transgender are more historically recent, and some are still not yet recognized in all jurisdictions. Other grounds, such as some of those set out in the United Nations Universal Declaration of Human Rights, language, political or other opinion, national or social origin, property, birth or other status, are still not implemented in many of the existing national discrimination laws. The following brief account is based on the legal instruments adopted with respect to the historical development of legal discrimination protections in certain jurisdictions, and cannot be seen as reflecting all the heroic efforts made by the many different groups of individuals throughout modern times.

## Part 1: Modern International Historical Developments as to Discrimination Issues

Modern international efforts with respect to issues related to discrimination protections can be seen as having two phases: ad hoc national efforts striving for international cooperations prior to World War I, and the stronger cohesive international approach as taken by the League of Nations, the International Labour Organization and the United Nations in the aftermaths of the two World Wars.[1] Initial modern endeavors addressing issues of discrimination were in response to the exploitation of human labor in the forms of slavery, forced labor and servitude, an exploitation that has been perpetual and endemic even to the present day. In the modern Western perspective, the Atlantic slave trade[2] added a new aspect to this historical phenomenon that made it a particularly egregious form, an industrialization of the institution of slavery. An estimated 12.5 million individuals were taken from Africa between 1514 to 1866 in the slave trade conducted by flagged ships in today's Brazil, Denmark, France, Germany, The Netherlands, Norway, Portugal, Spain, Sweden, the

1 For a longer historical overview, *see* Micheline R. Ishay, THE HISTORY OF HUMAN RIGHTS FROM ANCIENT TIMES TO THE GLOBALIZATION ERA (2nd ed. Univ. of California Press 2008) and Samuel Moyn, HUMAN RIGHTS AND THE USES OF HISTORY: EXPANDED (2nd ed. Verso 2017).

2 Two other forms of slave trade were present in 19th century Africa, White Slave Trade involving captured European seamen, and Oriental Slave Trade directed mainly at customers from the Middle East and Northern Africa, *see* Jean Allain, THE LAW AND SLAVERY, PROHIBITING HUMAN EXPLOITATION 39 (Brill 2015).

United Kingdom, the United States, and Uruguay.[3] Legislation as to banning the slave trade was proposed in Great Britain as early as 1776,[4] and in the passing of the 1806 domestic ban, Lord Grenville characterized slavery as contrary to the rights of nature, whereby "every human being is entitled to the fruit of his own labor."[5]

Great Britain worked thereafter for the international abolition of the slave trade at sea. This was controversial not only due to the actual abolition of slavery and the slave trade, but as it also involved issues of sovereignty and freedom of the seas.[6] The British demand for a declaration that engaging in the slave trade was piracy necessitated the right to check ships for slave contraband. The other European countries were not willing to concede such limitations, resulting in a very diluted Declaration on the Abolition of the Slave Trade by the Congress of Vienna in 1815, expressing the wish of "putting an end to the scourge, which has so long desolated Africa, degraded Europe and afflicted humanity."[7] The failure to reach an international agreement led the British to enter into a system of bilateral international agreements for the purpose of ending the Atlantic slave trade.[8] The signatories to the 1885 General

---

3 Allain 6.

4 Historically, Great Britain, Portugal and France accounted for 90% of the Atlantic slave trade, *see* Keith Bradley and Paul Cartledge, THE CAMBRIDGE WORLD HISTORY OF SLAVERY 583 (Cambridge Univ. Press 2011).

5 *See* Jenny Martinez, THE SLAVE TRADE AND THE ORIGINS OF INTERNATIONAL HUMAN RIGHTS LAW 17 (OUP 2012). In *Somerset v. Stewart*, 98 ER 499 (1772), the English Court of King's Bench held that slavery was not recognized within Britain and consequently the status of slave as to any person brought into Britain was not recognized, with Lord Mansfield finding that the law favored freedom.

6 Slavery as an institution historically was regulated by *ius gentium* during Roman times, then later by the law of nations, as slaves typically were captured in war, *see* Martinez 17.

7 Allain 4 *citing Declaration des 8 Cours, relative à l'Abolition Universelle de la Traite des Nègres*, Annex XV, 8 February 1815, BRITISH AND FOREIGN STATE PAPERS, VOL. 3, 972 (1815–1816). The signatories were Austria, Britain, France, Prussia, Russia, Portugal, Spain and Sweden-Norway.

8 The UK banned the slave trade first partially with the 1788 Slave Trade Act (Dolben's Act), 28 Geo. 3, c. 54. and then completely with the Slave Trade Act 1807, Geo. 3, Sess 1 c. 36. Slavery was outlawed by legislation in the UK and all its colonies in 1833. The UK was successful in negotiating bilateral treaties with Portugal (1810), Sweden (1813), Denmark (1814 which had already outlawed slave trade in 1792 effective 1803), France (1814 effective 1826), Spain (1814), The Netherlands (1814) and the United States (1814). Slavery however was outlawed in these countries at different times, Portugal (1761 domestically, 1858 in its colonies), Sweden (1335 domestically, 1847 in all Swedish possessions), Denmark (1846), France (1848), Spain (1811 including its colonies), The Netherlands (1861) and the United States (1865). Canada was

Act of Berlin regulating Europe's colonization of Africa resolved to end slavery by African and Islamic powers, however still very much a soft law approach to slavery while at the same time, a hard law approach to divvying up the African continent. It was not until the General Act of the Brussels Conference of 1890[9] that European countries conceded certain rights as to the freedom of the seas, constituting the first binding international legal document against the slave trade. Conventions regarding the suppression of White Slave traffic were signed in 1904 and 1910 targeting sex and labor trafficking in women and children.

A similar "industrialization" of labor led to a struggle for emancipation by workers, with demands for labor reforms during this same period. The origins of an international labor movement are traced to 1818 meetings of states at Frankfurter and Aix-la-Chapelle. Robert Owen, already active in British labor reform, argued unsuccessfully at both meetings that a prime task for American and European governments was the international fixation of legal limits of normal industrial conditions.[10] Two decades later, Daniel Legrand proposed a European cooperation for industrial welfare. Legrand had compiled by the 1850's a list of labor issues that needed to be addressed internationally, including providing elementary schools, instruction for young workers up to confirmation, Sunday schools, Sunday rest, the encouragement of family life, universal savings banks, old-age pensions, as well as prohibitions against child labor, excessive labor and night work.

The International Workingmen's Association, later the First International Labour Federation, was founded in London in 1864, with Karl Marx a member

---

the first British colony to abolish slavery with An Act to Prevent the further Introduction of Slaves and to limit the Term of Contracts for Servitude within this Province in 1793. German participation in the Atlantic slave trade is difficult to trace as it was not unified as a nation until 1870, but for information on Germany and the slave trade, *see* Andrea Weindl, Chapter 9 *The Slave Trade of Northern Germany from the Seventeenth to the Nineteenth Centuries* in David Eltis and David Richardson (eds.), EXTENDING THE FRONTIERS, ESSAYS ON THE NEW TRANSATLANTIC SLAVE TRADE DATABASE 250 (Yale 2008).

9 The Convention Relative to the Slave Trade and Importation into Africa of Firearms, Ammunition, and Spiritous Liquors of 1890, covering the slave trade at both sea and land. The States Parties were the United Kingdom, France, the German Empire, the Kingdom of Portugal, the Congo Free State, the Kingdom of Italy, The Kingdom of Spain, the Netherlands, Belgium, the Russian Empire, Austria-Hungary, Sweden-Norway, Denmark, the United States, the Ottoman Empire, Zanzibar and Persia.

10 *See* Robert Owen, TWO MEMORIALS ON BEHALF OF THE WORKING CLASSES: THE FIRST PRESENTED TO THE GOVERNMENTS OF EUROPE AND AMERICA, THE SECOND TO THE ALLIED POWERS ASSEMBLED IN CONGRESS AT AIX-LA-CHAPELLE (London 1818). *See also* Boutelle Lowe, INTERNATIONAL ASPECTS OF THE LABOR PROBLEM 5–10 (Columbia Univ. 1918).

of its General Council. Proposals were made two years later at its first congress in Geneva regarding restricting child labor, maximum working hours, and a prohibition of night work particularly for women.[11] The 1890 Berlin international labor conference, convened at the initiative of German Emperor Wilhelm II, addressed the work of women, children and young persons, Sunday labor and mining.[12] The International Association for Labour Legislation was founded in Paris in 1900 and its International Labour Office had the mission to publish, in French, German and English, the labor legislation of all countries and draft proposals as to labor legislation.[13] The first of these drafts to result in concrete action concerned women's night work, the 1905 Berne Convention. It became the first international regulation of labor entering into force in 1912, hailed as "one of the most glorious pages in the social history of nations."[14]

Women had also been fighting for emancipation from fathers and husbands through the grant of legal capacity, the right to vote and to compete in the labor market on the same terms as men. That women were the object of the first international labor regulation was not viewed by most women's groups as progress. Many women's groups were against the night work restrictions as impeding women's efforts to attain equality with men in employment and public life. The two arguments cited as bases for the convention, the care of present and future generations, and a consideration of women's generally weaker body constitutions in comparison to men's, were not seen as compelling. These groups maintained that there was no need to so significantly limit women's freedom of work. Night work was harmful to both sexes, with no evidence that it was more harmful to women. A better solution would be to increase wages generally to compensate for the negative effects of night work, as it occurred most frequently in low wage sectors.[15] The night work debate took on another

---

11 Helga Grebing, HISTORY OF THE GERMAN LABOUR MOVEMENT—A SURVEY 47 (Berg Publishing 1969). *See also* Marcello Musto, *Notes on the History of the International*, 28:2 SOCIALISM AND DEMOCRACY 5–38 (2014).

12 The countries represented were Germany, France, Austria-Hungary, England, Holland, Spain, Switzerland, Norway, Sweden, Portugal, Denmark, Belgium, Italy and Luxemburg.

13 *See* Report of the Committee of Experts, Report International Labor Conference 89th session 3 of the Report III (1B)-2001—*Chapter 2 Anatomy of a Prohibition: ILO Standards in Relation to Night Work of Women in Industry* 24 (ILO 2001).

14 The signatories were Austria, Belgium, France, Germany, Great Britain, Italy, Netherlands, Portugal, Spain, Sweden and Switzerland, *see* id. 27 and the Report of the Committee of Experts, Report International Labor Conference 89th, 27. The second international labor regulation was adopted the next year, the 1906 Berne International Convention respecting the Prohibition of the Use of White Phosphorus in the Manufacture of Matches.

15 Ruth Bohman, KVINNOR I FACKLIG OCH POLITISK KAMP 1880–1920: KRING BORGERLIGA OCH PROLETÄRA KVINNORÖRELSER I SVERIGE 33 (Zenit Häften 2 1979).

dimension in the 1900's due to employment competition between male and female workers. Women's wages were half those of their male counterparts in certain industries, creating a greater demand for women workers: "One must always with sympathy favor laws that drive women away from the labor market. If there were no women in the factories, unemployment would not be so great."[16] The objectives of women's groups at this time, legal capacity, voting rights and equality, were not addressed by any legal international efforts.

### *World War I and the ILO: A Wild Dream*

World War I marked the beginning of a new type of warfare, an industrialization so to speak of killing. Three peace treaties were signed to bring the war to a close, the Treaty of Versailles,[17] Saint-Germain-en-Laye[18] and Trianon.[19] All three peace treaties went beyond simply terms of peace, addressing issues of slavery, labor and discrimination law in efforts to address social unrest and reduce the risks of future wars. These treaties confirmed the 1890 General Act of Brussels, the 1906 convention on the suppression of night work for women, the 1904 and 1910 conventions against white slave traffic, as well as the Covenant of the League of Nations. Under the Covenant, the members of the League agreed to secure and maintain fair and humane conditions of labor for men, women and children, both domestically and through trade, secure the just treatment of native inhabitants of territories under their control, and entrust the League with the execution of agreements with regard to traffic in women

16 *Id.* 32. The effects of the night work ban were devastating for women in certain industries and countries. When the ban was passed in 1910 in Sweden, there were approximately 500 female typographers, a typical female night work, by 1934 only four women remained in the sector, *see* Bohman 34 *citing* Arbetets kvinnor 1934. The ILO Night Work (Women) Convention, 1919 (No. 4), Night Work (Bakeries) Convention, 1925 (No. 20), and Night Work (Women) Convention (Revised), 1934 (No. 41) are all now shelved by the ILO, with the present ILO Night Work Convention, 1990 (No. 171) applicable to both men and women.

17 The Treaty of Peace between the Allied and Associated Powers and Germany, the Protocol annexed thereto, the Agreement respecting the military occupation of the territories of the Rhine, and the Treaty between France and Great Britain respecting assistance to France in the event of unprovoked aggression by Germany, signed at Versailles on June 28, 1919.

18 Treaty of Peace between the Allied and Associated Powers and Austria together with the Protocol and Declarations Annexed Thereto signed at Saint-German-en-Laye on September 10, 1919. Austria agreed to be bound by the 1890 Brussels Act under Article 373 of the treaty.

19 Treaty of Peace Between the Allied and Associated Powers and Hungary and Protocol and Declaration, Signed at Trianon on June 4, 1920.

and children. The articles founding the League also stated that positions with the League were to be equally open to men and women. These protections in the Covenant are seen as the inception of both minority rights and international human rights law.[20]

In the continued effort to combat slavery, the League adopted the 1926 Slavery Convention, referring to the General Act of Berlin of 1885, the General Act of the Brussels Conference of 1890 declaring the "firm intention of putting an end to the traffic in African slaves," and the Convention of Saint-Germain-en-Laye of 1919. The signatories agreed to undertake to prevent and suppress the slave trade, and to "bring about, progressively and as soon as possible, the complete abolition of slavery in all its forms."[21] They also raised the necessity of preventing "forced labour from developing into conditions analogous to slavery". Almost a century after the system of British bilateral slave trade treaties was put in place, the 1926 Convention still addressed issues of the law of the seas, with the contracting parties undertaking "to adopt all appropriate measures with a view to preventing and suppressing the embarkation, disembarkation and transport of slaves in their territorial waters and upon all vessels flying their respective flags."[22]

The 1919 Treaty of Versailles set out the first meeting of an annual labor conference to be held that same year, in essence the foundation of the International Labour Organization ("ILO"). The ILO[23] was created in recognition of the fact that "conditions of labour exist involving such injustice, hardship and privation to large numbers of people as to produce unrest so great that the peace and harmony of the world are imperilled."[24] Stating in the ILO General Principles that labor should not be regarded merely as an article of commerce, certain issues were deemed of special and urgent importance, including a living wage, limitations as to working times, a right to rest, and the principle that men and women should receive equal remuneration for work of equal value.[25]

The ILO Constitution was drafted by a Labour Commission chaired by Samuel Gompers, the head of the American Federation of Labor in the United

---

20 *See* Malcolm Shaw, INTERNATIONAL LAW 270 (6th ed. Cambridge 2008).

21 Article 2, Slavery Convention Signed at Geneva on 25 September 1926.

22 *Id.* Article 3.

23 After World War II, the ILO became a specialized agency of the UN in 1946, and currently has 185 members.

24 Part XIII. Labour, Section 1, Organisation of Labour, Ingress. *See also* ILO, RULES OF THE GAME, A BRIEF INTRODUCTION TO INTERNATIONAL LABOUR STANDARDS 9 (2014).

25 Article 395 stated that the staff of the ILO was to represent different nationalities and include women.

States, and composed of representatives from nine countries: Belgium, Cuba, Czechoslovakia, France, Italy, Japan, Poland, the United Kingdom and the United States. A tripartite organization was created for the ILO, comprising representatives of governments, employers and workers in the ILO executive bodies. Inspiration for the constitution was gathered from the work done by the International Association for Labour Legislation.[26] President Franklin Roosevelt, when discussing the origins of the ILO, reminisced:

> I well remember that in those days the ILO was still a dream. To many it was a wild dream. Who had ever heard of Governments getting together to raise the standards of labor on an international plan? Wilder still was the idea that the people themselves who were directly affected—the workers and the employers of the various countries—should have had a hand with Government in determining these labor standards.[27]

Six conventions were adopted at this first 1919 meeting, creating international labor standards for hours of work in industry, unemployment, maternity protections, night work for women, minimum age requirements and night work for young persons in industry.

Ending unfair discrimination at work is still currently one of the four fundamental policies set out in the ILO 1998 Declaration on Fundamental Principles and Rights at Work, as supported by two core conventions, the Equal Remuneration Convention, 1951 (No. 100) and the Discrimination (Employment and Occupation) Convention, 1958 (No. 111).[28] General employment discrimination protections are set out in the 1958 Discrimination (Employment and Occupation) Convention, defining discrimination in its Article 1 as "any distinction,

26 For this history, *see* the ILO website, ilo.org under the section, About the ILO and Origins and History.

27 Gerry Rodgers, Eddy Lee, Lee Swepston and Jasmien Van Daele, THE INTERNATIONAL LABOUR ORGANIZATION AND THE QUEST FOR SOCIAL JUSTICE 1919–2009 1 (ILO 2009).

28 ILO, RULES OF THE GAME 15. The other three fundamental policies, each supported by two core Conventions are: The right of workers to associate freely and bargain collectively [supported by the Freedom of Association and Protection of the Right to Organise Convention, 1948 (No. 87) and the Right to Organise and Collective Bargaining Convention, 1951 (No. 98)]; the eradication of forced labour 8 [supported by the Forced Labour Convention, 1930 (No. 29) and the Abolition of Forced Labour Convention, 1957 (No. 105)]; and the abolition of child labour [supported by the Minimum Age Convention, 1973 (No. 138) and the Worst Forms of Child Labour Convention, 1999 (No. 182)]. There are currently over 1,357 ratifications of these in total eight core conventions supporting these four policies, representing 91.7% of the possible number of ratifications.

exclusion or preference made on the basis of race, colour, sex, religion, political opinion, national extraction or social origin, which has the effect of nullifying or impairing equality of opportunity or treatment in employment or occupation." Specific discrimination topics are addressed in several of the almost 190 ILO conventions to-date, including for example, equal remuneration, social benefits,[29] maternity,[30] gender in combining work and family[31] part-time work[32] and domestic work[33] as well as equality of treatment for indigenous workers,[34] migrants and non-nationals,[35] and individuals with disabilities.[36]

### *World War II and the UN*

The atrocities committed under Hitler and the Nazi regime against the Jews,[37] Romani, homosexuals, labor leaders and many others, resulted in significant

---

29 ILO Equality of Treatment (Social Security) Convention, 1962 (No. 118) mandates equal treatment of nationals as to the provision of social welfare benefits.

30 ILO Maternity Protection Convention, 1919 (No. 3), Maternity Protection Convention (Revised), 1952 (No. 103) and now ILO Maternity Protection Convention, 2000 (No. 183).

31 ILO Workers with Families Responsibilities, 1981 (No. 156) addresses enabling workers with family responsibilities to combine such with employment.

32 ILO Part-time Work Convention, 1994 (No. 185) covers measures to be taken to ensure that part-time workers (predominantly women worldwide) receive the same protection as full-time workers.

33 ILO Domestic Workers Convention, 2011 (No. 189) protects the human rights of domestic workers.

34 ILO Contracts of Employment (Indigenous Workers) Convention, 1939 (No. 64), requiring employment contracts setting out certain terms as to wages and work for indigenous workers and ILO Indigenous and Tribal Peoples Convention, 1989 (No. 169) protects the rights of indigenous and tribal peoples to self-identification, recognition, equal treatment and respect for integrity.

35 ILO Migration for Employment Convention, 1939 (No. 65) revised by ILO Migration for Employment Convention, Revised 1949 (No. 97) sets out requirements for an equal treatment of migrants, irrespective of nationality, race, religion or sex, with rights for example to health services, information, fair wages, trade union membership and social security. ILO Migrant Workers (Supplementary Provisions) Convention, 1975 (No. 143) requires employers to respect the basic human rights of all migrant workers. *See also* the ILO Equality of Treatment (Accident Compensation) Convention, 1925 (No. 19), mandating equal treatment of nationals and foreigners with respect to occupational hazard insurance.

36 The Vocational Rehabilitation and Employment (Disable Persons) Convention, 1983 (No. 159) sets out rights for disable persons to engage in vocational rehabilitation.

37 Many of these groups had been consistently persecuted throughout the Middle Ages up to modern times. Under medieval law, which was mostly local city or countryside law, as nations as such did not exist until later, distinctions were made as to strangers, foreigners (based on *forren* from the Medieval Latin *forinseci*) and aliens. Strangers and foreigners were simply outsiders, persons not born or apprenticed within a specific town or village.

post-war legal instruments protecting human rights and providing discrimination protections. The United Nations Declaration was signed on New Year's Day 1942 by the United States, the United Kingdom, the Soviet Union and China. Representatives of twenty-two countries still fighting the Rome-Berlin-Tokyo Axis signed the declaration the next day. The United Nations ("UN") as an organization was founded three years later under the 1945 Charter of the United Nations and the Statute of the International Court of Justice. The 1948 United Nations Universal Declaration of Human Rights ("UNDHR") was proclaimed by the United Nations General Assembly[38] as a common standard of achievements for all peoples and all nations as the "recognition of the inherent dignity and of the equal and inalienable rights of all members of the human family is the foundation of freedom, justice and peace in the world," and that fundamental human rights must be universally protected under the rule of law.

Protections against discrimination are set out in Article 2 UNDHR:

> Everyone is entitled to all the rights and freedoms set forth in this Declaration, without distinction of any kind, such as race, colour, sex, language, religion, political or other opinion, national or social origin, property, birth or other status. Furthermore, no distinction shall be made on the basis of the political, jurisdictional or international status of the country or territory to which a person belongs, whether it be independent, trust, non-self-governing or under any other limitation of sovereignty.

Everyone is to have the right to life, liberty and security of person (Article 3) and no one is to be held in slavery or servitude, slavery and the slave trade are to be prohibited in all their forms (Article 4). Every individual is to have the right to recognition everywhere as a person before the law (Article 6), and all are to be equal before the law, entitled without discrimination to the equal protection of the law, including as to any discrimination suffered in violation of the UNDHR (Article 7). Equal rights to effective judicial remedies, fair and public hearings by independent and impartial tribunals, to be presumed innocent until guilty, to be free of arbitrary interference with privacy, family home and correspondence are set out in articles 8–12. Rights to free movement, asylum, nationality, marriage, family and property are granted in articles 13–17.

---

Someone from beyond the sea was an alien. All three categories lacked the protection of the local laws. Certain groups were also systematically mistreated societally and by law beginning already during the middle ages, such as the Jews, Romani and homosexuals.

38 United Nations General Assembly Resolution 217 A.

Freedom of thought, conscience and religion, opinion and expression, as well as political participation, are protected in articles 18–21. Protections as to social welfare, education, culture, the right of association and the rights to work, to equal pay, fair labor conditions, and leisure are provided by articles 22–29.

The UN amended the 1926 Slavery Convention by Protocol in 1953. A UN 1956 Supplementary Convention on the Abolition of Slavery, the Slave Trade, and Institutions and Practices Similar to Slavery was adopted, beginning with the statement that "freedom is the birthright of every human being." Finding that slavery still existed, the 1956 Convention called for its immediate abolition, as well as that of debt bondage, serfdom, and any institution or practice whereby women or children are married, transferred or inherited by families. The next year the ILO adopted the 1957 Abolition of Forced Labour Convention.

Three significant UN human rights documents were promulgated by the UN in the 1960's, the 1965 International Convention on the Elimination of All Forms of Racial Discrimination ("ICERD"), the 1966 International Covenant on Civil and Political Rights ("ICCPR") and the 1966 International Covenant on Economic, Social and Cultural Rights ("ICESCR").[39] These three instruments reaffirm and at times expand many of the protections in the UNDHR, and are seen as reflecting first, second and third generation human rights.[40] ICERD focuses on protections from racial discrimination defined as "any distinction, exclusion, restriction or preference based on race, colour, descent, or national or ethnic origin which has the purpose or effect of nullifying or impairing the recognition, enjoyment or exercise, on an equal footing, of human rights and fundamental freedoms in the political, economic, social, cultural or any other field of public life." The ICCPR and ICESCR are twin documents, with the ICCPR covering civil and political rights, most of which are negative rights in

39 *See* Sandra Fredman and Meghan Campbell, SOCIAL AND ECONOMIC RIGHTS AND CONSTITUTIONAL LAW (Edward Elgar 2016).

40 This taxology was set out by Karel Vasak in his article, *Human Rights: A Thirty-Year Struggle: the Sustained Efforts to give Force of law to the Universal Declaration of Human Rights*, 30 (11) UNESCO COURIER 29 (Paris United Nations Educational, Scientific and Cultural Organisation/UNESCO 1977). First generation human rights are negative rights, prohibitions as to state action. These are often liberal rights concerning the citizen and the state, civic and political. Second generation human rights are positive rights requiring state action, usually economic, social and cultural in nature, such as rights to housing. Third generation human rights are often group and collective rights, which Vasak referred to as rights of solidarity, *citing* UNESCO Director-General Amadou-Mahtar M'Bow. Third-generation rights are to a certain conception of community life, for example, a healthy and ecologically-balanced environment.

that the state is not to infringe upon them, such as protection from cruel and inhuman treatment. The ICESCR sets out economic, social and cultural rights, positive rights for example as to housing, which the state is to enable. Both ICCPR and ICESCR rights are to be granted without distinctions of any kind as to race, colour, sex, language, religion, political or other opinion, national or social origin, property, birth or other status. This system of twin documents serves as a model for several of the regional human rights instruments, including those of the Council of Europe and the Organization of American States as described in the next parts.

In the next decades, the UN conventions concerning discrimination protections addressed specific groups: women, children, migrant workers, and persons with disabilities. The 1979 Convention of the Elimination of All Forms of Discrimination against Women ("CEDAW") defines the term "discrimination against women" in its Article 1 as "any distinction, exclusion or restriction made on the basis of sex which has the effect or purpose of impairing or nullifying the recognition, enjoyment or exercise by women, irrespective of their marital status, on a basis of equality of men and women, of human rights and fundamental freedoms in the political, economic, social, cultural, civil or any other field." Civil rights and the legal status of women, as well as human reproduction and the impact of cultural factors on gender relations are taken up in CEDAW.[41]

The 1989 Convention on the Rights of the Child ("CRC") sets out the principle of the "best interests of the child" that is to govern state interaction with children, including providing children with such protection and care as necessary for their well-being. States are to ensure and respect the CRC rights of each child within their jurisdiction and "without discrimination of any kind, irrespective of the child's or his or her parent's or legal guardian's race, colour, sex, language, religion, political or other opinion, national, ethnic or social origin, property, disability, birth or other status."

The 1990 International Convention on the Protection of the Rights of All Migrant Workers and Members of Their Families ("CMW") aims to ensure that migrant workers and their families enjoy freedom of movement, the right to life, to humane treatment, and to not be held in slavery, servitude, forced or compulsory labor. Migrant workers are to have the full protection of their human rights, regardless of their legal status, sex, race, color, language, religion or conviction, political or other opinion, national, ethnic or social origin,

41 CEDAW has been criticized for its focus on simply women, instead of on gender, *see e.g.*, Darren Rosenblum, *Unsex Cedaw, or What's Wrong with Women's Rights*, 20 COLUMBIA J. GENDER AND LAW 98–194 (2011).

nationality, age, economic position, property, marital status, birth or other status.

The 2006 Convention on the Rights of Person with Disabilities ("CRPD") was adopted as stated in its Article 1 to "promote, protect and ensure the full and equal enjoyment of all human rights and fundamental freedoms by all persons with disabilities, and to promote respect for their inherent dignity." Persons with disabilities are defined as those who have long-term physical, mental, intellectual or sensory impairments which in interaction with various barriers may hinder their full and effective participation in society on an equal basis with others. Eight guiding principles underlie the Convention as stated in Article 3 CRPD:

- Respect for inherent dignity, individual autonomy including the freedom to make one's own choices, and independence of persons;
- Non-discrimination;
- Full and effective participation and inclusion in society;
- Respect for difference and acceptance of persons with disabilities as part of human diversity and humanity;
- Equality of opportunity;
- Accessibility;
- Equality between men and women; and
- Respect for the evolving capacities of children with disabilities and respect for the right of children with disabilities to preserve their identities.

The Convention requires in Article 5 that States Parties recognize that all persons are equal before and under the law and are entitled without any discrimination to the equal protection and equal benefit of the law. All discrimination on the basis of disability is to be prohibited and the States Parties are to guarantee to persons with disabilities equal and effective legal protection against discrimination on all grounds. Reasonable accommodation is to be provided to promote equality and eliminate discrimination. Article 6 sets out specific protections for women and girls with disabilities as they are seen more often to be subject to "multiple discrimination."

A development in these different international legal instruments can be traced during this period with respect to both sophistication and strength of conviction as to eradicating discrimination. Beginning with the issue of slave trade and state sovereignty at the turn of the 19th century, a greater understanding of emancipation and equality is evidenced in the more recent international instruments, particularly the CRPD as evidenced by the eight guiding principles. Issues of slavery, servitude, indentureship, compulsory and forced labor, as well as trafficking, are still very much with us today, as evidence by the 2014 ILO Forced Labour Protocol to the 1930 convention, issued to combat forced labor, modern slavery and human trafficking. The vulnerability of the rights granted under these international treaties and conventions is that they are public international law documents. In countries adopting a dualistic approach to international law documents, this means that the treaties are binding on the States Parties with respect to each other. For example, State A one can sue State B for State B's violation of the treaty. However, these treaties concern the rights of individuals. Individuals can only legally claim rights under these treaties if their state has incorporated the treaty into domestic law. If the state has failed to incorporate the treaty into national law, courts can still invoke the terms of the treaty as a way to interpret national law. An individual cannot make a claim in a national court on the basis of a treaty that has not been incorporated into the national law under the system of dualism. In a completely monistic state, any international legal obligation is treated the same as national legislation without any requirement of incorporation and the individual can directly cite the treaty as a basis for a claim in the national courts. The vast majority of countries have adopted the dualism approach, entailing that individuals are very much dependent upon their governments taking the obligations set out in these legal instruments seriously, incorporating them into national laws that can be invoked before courts.

A limited expansion of the protected grounds in the international human rights instruments can be detected (see appendix one). Explicit protections with respect to unlawful discrimination based on age or LGBTQUIA (lesbian, gay, bisexual, transgender, queer and questioning, intersex and intergender and anonymous and ally) grounds have yet to be given. The Yogyakarta Principles on the Application of International Human Rights Law in relation to Sexual Orientation and Gender Identity were drafted as a response to this lacuna, articulating a set of twenty-nine principles applying international human rights law to address the abuse of the human rights of lesbian, gay, bisexual, transgender and intersexed individuals. These principles were drafted in 2006 at a meeting of the International Commission of Jurists, the International Service for Human Rights and human rights experts. As they are not integrated into a treaty, they are not binding, but clearly demonstrate the need for such international discrimination protections in this area.[42]

42 For more information on the Yogyakarta Principles, *see* yogyakartaprinciples.org.

## Part 2: The Europeanisation of Discrimination Protections

The Council of Europe ("COE") and the European Union ("EU"), distinct but intertwined regional cooperations, are addressed in this part separately from the other regional cooperations due to their unique nature. In contrast to the regional entities discussed in Part 3, the EU combines both international instruments in the form of treaties binding between the Member States as international law documents,[43] as well as internally promulgated instruments such as regulations, directives and case law, also binding on the Member States. EU regulations automatically become the law of the Member States upon their adoption at the EU level, while directives set out implementation periods during which the Member States are to transform the requirements of the EU directive into national law, similar to the dualistic system discussed in the previous part. The duty of loyalty, a general principle of Union law, ensures a substantive, and not just formal, compliance by the Member States. The failure of a member state to implement Union law is a violation of its EU treaty obligations, and can be sanctioned in the forms of warnings, fines, and theoretically, expulsion. The reach of EU law consequently is stronger as well as deeper than that of typical international or regional legal instruments.[44]

### *The Council of Europe*

The Council of Europe was established through the 1949 Treaty of London by its ten founders, Belgium, Denmark, France, Ireland, Italy, Luxembourg, the Netherlands, Norway, Sweden and the United Kingdom, with Greece, Turkey, Iceland and West Germany joining by the next year. COE currently has forty-seven members. COE drafted both the 1950 European Convention for the Protection of Human Rights and Fundamental Freedoms[45] and the European Social Charter of 1961 guaranteeing social and economic rights to give effect to the United Nations Universal Declaration of Human Rights. Certain rights are

---

43 The two main EU treaties after Lisbon are TEU (originally the "Treaty of Maastricht" signed in 1992) and TFEU (originally the "Treaty of Rome", the "Treaty establishing the European Economic Community" or the "EEC Treaty" signed in 1957). Both treaties are updated and issued in their consolidated forms, available at the EU law website, eur-lex.europa.eu.

44 Given the requirements of harmonization, the argument can be made that the EU has very significant powers, in some respects even greater than those for example of the United States federal government, which cannot require the different US states to harmonize their state legislation.

45 Referred to as the "European Convention" or the "ECHR." For more information on the ECHR, *see* the Council's website, coe.int.

protected within both instruments, such as prohibitions as to slavery, forced labor, inhumane and degrading treatment, and the rights to life, health, the environment, privacy, education, family and employment protections including trade union rights.

The European Convention was signed in Rome in 1950 by the COE founders. Under its Article 14, the signatories commit to that "[t]he enjoyment of the rights and freedoms set forth in this Convention shall be secured without discrimination on any ground such as sex, race, colour, language, religion, political or other opinion, national or social origin, association with a national minority, property, birth or other status." Two additional acts are required by the signatories for the implementation of the system regarding the protections under the European Convention, recognition of the Council's jurisdiction to receive individual applications and a declaration by the member accepting the jurisdiction of the European Court of Human Rights ("ECtHR") in Strasbourg. Applications concerning violations of the ECHR and its protocols can be lodged with the ECtHR by individuals within six months after exhausting available national remedies. The member countries found in violation of the ECHR are under an obligation to comply with the Court's judgment.

The European Social Charter of 1961 protects the enjoyment of social rights, which are to be secured without any discrimination on the grounds of race, color, sex, religion, political opinion, national extraction or social origin. Included in the rights recognized are those to fair remuneration and equal pay between men and women for work of equal value, the right for women to take parental leave without retaliation, general rights to social assistance and welfare, as well as specific rights for mothers, children, migrant workers and their families, and individuals with disabilities.

The 1961 Charter was revised in 1996, and several articles in the 1996 Revised Charter address equal treatment, including the right to equal opportunities and equal treatment in matters of employment and occupation without discrimination on the grounds of sex (Article 20) and the right to reconcile work and family life "without being subject to discrimination and as far as possible without conflict between their employment and family responsibilities" (Article 27). A general principle of non-discrimination is contained in Article E of the Revised Charter, stating that the enjoyment of the Charter rights are to be secured without discrimination on any ground such as "race, colour, sex, language, religion, political or other opinion, national extraction or social origin, health, association with a national minority, birth or other status."[46]

---

46 For a review of the discrimination case law of ECtHR and the CJEU, *see* European Union Agency for Fundamental Rights and the Council of Europe, Handbook on European

Consequently, the Revised Charter expands the list of protected grounds by adding language, other opinion, health, association with a national minority, birth or other status. The European Committee of Social Rights monitors compliance by the States Parties to the Charters through two channels, a States Parties reporting system and a collective complaint procedure available to the social partners and non-governmental organizations ("NGOs") where the Committee issues decisions.

All 28 EU Member States are COE member states, and all have signed the European Convention, the 1961 European Social Charter and the 1996 European Social Charter (Revised).[47] Prior to the 2009 Treaty of Lisbon, the EU could not sign the European Convention as the EU was neither a legal person nor a state. Under the Treaty of Lisbon, the EU is to accede under Article 6 TEU to the European Convention. However, the EU Court of Justice ("CJ") in a 2014 opinion held that the EU could not accede as then a body external to the EU, the European Court of Human Rights, would have the power to review and affect the application of EU law.[48]

### *The EU and Discrimination Protections*

Addressing social issues of any dimension was not foremost in the minds of the six drafters of the first of the treaties ultimately establishing the European Union, but rather the creation of an integrated Europe to insure future peace. The 1951 Treaty of the European Coal and Steel Community[49] created a common European market in coal and steel, and the first of the European Communities, the European Coal and Steel Community ("ECSC"). Belgium, France, the Federal Republic of Germany, Italy, Luxembourg and the Netherlands agreed that "world peace can be safeguarded only by creative efforts commensurate with the dangers that threaten it," and that Europe could "be built only through practical achievements which will first of all create real solidarity, and through the establishment of common bases for economic development."[50]

---

non-discrimination law (Luxembourg 2011) available online at the website of the EU Agency for Fundamental Rights, fra.europa.eu.

47 Thirty-five of the forty-seven COE member states have ratified the 1996 European Social Charter (Revised).

48 Opinion 2/13 [2014] ECLI:EU:C:2014:2454. This was the second time the Court had vetoed EU accession to the ECHR, for the first opinion, *see* Opinion 2/94 [1996] ECR 1759.

49 The Treaty establishing the European Coal and Steel Community ("ECSC Treaty"), was signed 18 April 1951, entered into force 24 July 1952 and expired 23 July 2003.

50 *See* the second and fourth paragraphs of the preamble to the ECSC Treaty. As of 2017, the twenty-eight Member States cover over five hundred million people in Europe. The UK had a popular referendum in 2016 resulting in a vote to leave the EU, "Brexit." Article 50 of

Six years later, the 1957 Treaty establishing the European Economic Community ("EEC") extended the common market sectors from simply coal and steel to all economic sectors in the Member States through the establishment of the four freedoms of movement of goods, persons, capital and services.[51] A Social Policy Title was included with common community policies in certain key areas to insure these freedoms of movement: common agricultural, transportation and commercial policies. A common European market operating at maximum efficiency with the removal of all market distortions was viewed as beneficial for everyone, consumers, workers and employers alike, and in turn, would strengthen the national economies of the Member States.

The European Court of Justice was initially reluctant to address human rights against this background of an economic cooperation. However, the Court began evaluating issues and treaty rights against a background of fundamental rights by the 1970's, particularly with respect to actions by Community institutions and Member States. The Court held that fundamental rights ranked as general principles of Community law based on two sources: the constitutional traditions of the Member States, as well as the international treaties entered into by the Member States, particularly the ECHR. The principle of equal pay between men and women had been included in Article 119 EEC Treaty,[52] but was an oddity in this treaty creating an economic cooperation. Prohibiting social dumping, a very economic reason, was the argument made by France for its inclusion as this market distortion of unequal pay was seen as an impediment to the free movement of goods.[53] The Court gave Article 119 direct effect

the Lisbon Treaty as to a UK withdrawal was triggered by the UK Prime Minister Theresa May in March 2017. Despite Brexit, the current laws in the UK are still, and many most likely will remain for some time, consistent with the requirements placed by Union law.

51 Also referred to as the "EEC Treaty" or the "Treaty of Rome". The common European economic market was to be achieved by 1970, expiring in 2009. After the 2007 Treaty of Lisbon, the EEC treaty is now the Treaty on the Functioning of the European Union ("TFEU"). The Treaty Establishing the European Atomic Energy Community ("Euratom") was also signed by the original six members in 1957 and Euratom is the only remaining European community after the Treaty of Lisbon.

52 Now Article 157 TFEU.

53 France had equal pay provisions in place since World War II and at that time, one of the smallest pay differentials between women and men, 7% as compared to up to 40% in Italy. France argued that it could not compete with the price of goods from countries in which women were paid less than men, *see* Catherine Barnard, EC EMPLOYMENT LAW 23 (Oxford 2000) *citing* Melitta Budiner, LE DROIT DE LA FEMME A L'ÉGALITÉ DE SALAIRE ET LA CONVENTION NO. 100 DE L'ORGANISATION INTERNATIONALE DU TRAVAIL

both vertically and horizontally[54] in *Defrenne II*, laying the groundwork work for the EU social platform, finding that:

> Article 119 forms part of the social objectives of the Community, which is not merely an economic union, but is at the same time intended, by common action, to ensure social progress and seek the constant improvement of the living and working conditions of their peoples, as is emphasized by the preamble to the Treaty.[55]

This statement was made at a time when the EEC was still very much an economic cooperation with few if any avowed social objectives, and Article 119 was commonly believed to not have any direct effect, let alone the horizontal direct effect given by the Court for the first time in the case. The Court went on to state that this "double aim, which is at once economic and social, shows that the principle of equal pay forms part of the foundations of the Community", laying the groundwork for the fundamental rights approach taken in later cases, as well as for the EU social platform. The summit of the reasoning espoused by the Court in *Defrenne II* can be seen as reached in the 2000 case of *Seivers*,[56] where the Court states that:

---

(Librairie Générale de Droit et de Jurisprudence, Paris 1975). The drafting of Article 119 was also inspired by ILO Equal Remuneration Convention, 1951 (No. 100) mandating equal pay between women and men for work of equal value, *see* Catherine Barnard, EU EMPLOYMENT LAW 254 (4th ed. Oxford 2012).

54 Direct effect is a principle of Union law to ensure implementation by the Member States, first established by the Court in Case 26/62, *Van Gend en Loos v. Nederlandse Administratie der Belastingen* [1963] ECR I-1. In essence, in the event a Member States has failed to implement EU legislation within the mandated period, or has impropely done so, the EU law will have direct effect in the Member State and can be cited by an individual as the basis for a legal claim. Vertical direct effect concerns claims by individuals against the state or public bodies, horizontal direct effect allows for claims by individuals against private parties. EU directives are not held to have horizontal direct effect, *see* Case 152/84, *Marshall v. Southampton and SW Hampshire AHA* [1986] ECR-723.

55 However, not retroactively from 1962 but rather from the date of the judgment, 1976, *see* Case C-43/75, *Gabriella Defrenne (No. 2) v. Societe Anonyme Belge de Navigation Aerienne Sabena* [1976] 1 ECR-455, para. 40. The Court's holding as to the non-retroactive application of Article 119 was in response to the arguments of Ireland and the UK that retroactivity from 1962 forward would expose many employers to claims of unequal pay spanning more than a decade, forcing many of them into bankruptcy, *see Defrenne* (No. 2) 480–81.

56 Case C-270/97, *Deutsche Post AG v. Elisabeth Sievers* [2000] ECR I-929.

> The economic aim pursued by Article 119 of the Treaty, namely the elimination of distortions of competition between undertakings established in different Member States, is secondary to the social aim pursued by the same provision, which constitutes the expression of a fundamental human right, namely, a person's right not to suffer discrimination on grounds of sex.

Almost twenty years after the adoption of the equal pay provision in Article 119, two triads of directives[57] were issued by the Council, the first addressing issues of sex discrimination in employment with respect to equal pay (75/117/EEC), equal treatment (76/207/EEC) and social security benefits (79/7/EEC). The second triad of directives was adopted to protect the rights of the most vulnerable workers during the then current economic recession, workers in situations of collective redundancies (75/129/EEC), transfers of undertakings (77/187/EEC), and employer insolvencies (80/987/EEC). The EU at this stage took a very *ad hoc* approach to discrimination and employment issues.

The European Parliament, the Commission and the Council signed a Joint Declaration in 1977 in which they undertook to continue to respect fundamental rights as arising from the two sources as identified by the Court, the constitutional traditions of the Member States as well as the ECHR. From the platform of the common market, the treaties began to incorporate social and political areas following the lead of the Court. Article 6 TEU now explicitly states that "[t]he Union is founded on the principles of liberty, democracy, respect for human rights and fundamental freedoms, and the rule of law, principles which are common to the Member States." The Union is also to "respect fundamental rights, as guaranteed by the European Convention ... and as they result from the constitutional traditions common to the Member States, as general principles of Community law."[58]

Recognition of the 1961 Social Charter was timid in the 1987 Single European Act which started the transformation of the common European market to a single European market. The Community Charter of Fundamental Social Rights of Workers was adopted in 1989 by declaration of all the Member States (thus not binding) with the exception initially of the United Kingdom, which acceded to it in 1997. Under the 1989 Charter, the Member States agreed that

57 These directives were the result of the Council's 1974 Action Programme, drawn up in response to the then existing period of social unrest and economic recession in Western Europe, *see* Council Resolution of 21 January 1974 concerning a social action programme, OJ 1974 C 13/1.

58 *See* Article 6(1) and (2) TEU, formerly Article F.2 EU Treaty.

to ensure equal treatment in the internal market, "it is important to combat every form of discrimination, including discrimination on grounds of sex, colour, race, opinions and beliefs, and whereas, in a spirit of solidarity, it is important to combat social exclusion." Fundamental social rights of workers are included, such as freely chosen employment and fair remuneration (Articles 4 to 6), equal treatment for men and women (Article 16), protection of children and adolescents at work (Articles 20 to 23), sufficient resources for the elderly upon retirement (Articles 24 to 25), and integration measures for persons with disabilities (Article 26).

The 1997 Amsterdam Treaty amended certain provisions of the European Community ("EC") Treaty with regard to discrimination and introduced a new "Title on Employment." Article 2 stated that "[t]he Community shall have as its task, by establishing a common market and an economic and monetary union and by implementing common policies ... to promote throughout the Community a harmonious, balanced and sustainable development of economic activities, a high level of employment and of social protection, equality between men and women, sustainable and non-inflationary growth ..."

Fundamental social rights were also a focus in the 1997 Amsterdam Treaty. Article 136 cited the 1961 Social Charter and the 1989 EU Charter, stating the objectives of the Union and Member States as "the promotion of employment, improved living and working conditions, so as to make possible their harmonisation while the improvement is being maintained, proper social protection, dialogue between management and labour, the development of human resources with a view to lasting high employment and the combating of exclusion." Activities the Union is to pursue to achieve these objectives include the improvement of the working environment "to protect workers' health and safety, working conditions, social security and social protection of workers and equality between men and women with regard to labor market opportunities and treatment at work and combating social exclusion."[59]

Work began on a Charter of Fundamental Rights of the European Union ("EU Charter") in 1999, which became legally binding through the Treaty of Lisbon in 2009. The objective of the EU Charter is to clarify the rights of EU citizens by consolidating the rights already existing in other EU sources, including the treaties, case law and ECHR. The preamble states that: "The peoples of Europe, in creating an ever closer union among them, are resolved to share a peaceful future based on common values. Conscious of its spiritual and moral heritage, the Union is founded on the indivisible, universal values of

59 Now Articles 151 and 153 TFEU respectively.

human dignity, freedom, equality and solidarity; it is based on the principles of democracy and the rule of law."

Structured in six chapters protecting dignity, freedoms, equality, solidarity, citizens' rights and justice respectively, its first article states that "[h]uman dignity is inviolable. It must be respected and protected." Slavery, servitude and forced labor are prohibited under Article 5. Part 3 addresses equality, with Article 20 stating that everyone is equal before the law. Any discrimination based on any ground such as sex, race, color, ethnic or social origin, genetic features, language, religion or belief, political or any other opinion, membership of a national minority, property, birth, disability, age or sexual orientation is prohibited under Article 21. Equality between women and men in employment, work and pay is prescribed in Article 23. Rights of children, the elderly and the integration of persons with disabilities are also set out in this chapter.

The development of discrimination protections within Union law initially was driven by the Court, followed by the EU legislature in the form of regulations and directives, and then by Member States in the treaties. Protections exist today in Union law with respect to discrimination on the basis of sex/gender, racial or ethnic origin, religion or belief, disability, age, gender reassignment and sexual orientation, still mostly in the area of employment, but under the social dimension, also in other areas. The current directives taking up issues of discrimination are the Pregnant Workers Directive 92/85/EC, Part-time Work 98/23/EC, Fixed Term Work 1999/70/EC, Racial Equality Directive 2000/43/EC (race and ethnic origins), Employment Equality Framework Directive 2000/78/EC (religion or belief, disability, age, gender reassignment and sexual orientation), the Equal Treatment Directive 2006/54/EC (sex), the Temporary and Agency Workers Directive 2008/104/EC and the Parental Leave Directive 2010/18/EU.

While the member states initially were given great discretion in choosing how to implement Union law requirements under the discrimination directives in the 1970's, there has been a greater requirement of access to justice for persons who have been discriminated in the implementation measures taken by member states. A shifted burden of proof was set out in the Burden of Proof Directive 97/80/EC, now incorporated in the discrimination directives, entailing that all the member states have to apply this burden of proof in the national court cases.[60] There is also now a heightened requirement of real and effective

60 The Court first invoked the shifted burden of proof in C-109/88, *Handels- og Kontorfunktionærernes Forbund i Danmark v. Dansk Arbejdsgiverforening, agissant pour Danfoss* [1989] ECR 3199, with the Burden of Proof Directive 97/80/EC following in 1997. For an assessment as to how the burden of proof is used at the EU and national levels, *see*

compensation or reparation for loss and damage sustained by a person injured as a result of discrimination, in a way that is dissuasive and proportionate to the damage suffered. Another requirement is for the Member States to have enforcement bodies as to these rights.

Violations of Union discrimination law, either after the national laws are harmonized or Union law has direct effect, are brought to the national courts. If the national court finds there is a question as to the interpretation or validity of Union law, the court can request a preliminary ruling from the Court to clarify the situation. Most of the cases addressing discrimination issues have been brought to the Court for preliminary rulings. The Court then only addresses the question of law as posed by the national courts, remanding the case back to the national court to apply Union law consistent with the Court's decision.

Examples of recent decisions by the Court in the area of discrimination law demonstrate both expansion and retraction of protections. The Court found that a discrimination case can be pursued without any requirement of a victim,[61] that a legal person can be responsible for an owner's homophobic statements,[62] and that persons harmed by, but not the target of, discriminatory practices were entitled to remedies.[63] These positive steps are counterbalanced by other CJ decisions, such as where the Court found that an employer's banning the wearing of an Islamic headscarf constituted neither direct nor indirect discrimination when the ban was based an internal company rule

---

European Commission, Reversing the burden of proof: Practical dilemmas at the European and national level (EU 2014), available at the website of the EU Commission, ec.europa.eu.

61 Case C-54–07, *Centrum voor Gelijkheid van Kansen en voor Rasismebestrijding v. NV Firma Ferijn* [2008] ECR 1390. In the case, a director publicly stated that the company did not want to hire immigrants because the customers were reluctant to give such persons access to their homes. The ECJ held that such a statement "being likely strongly to dissuade certain candidates from submitting their candidature and, accordingly, to hinder their access to the labour market, was in violation of the Race Directive 2000/43."

62 Case C-81/12 *Asociaţia Accept v. Consiliul Naţional pentru Combaterea Discriminării* [2013] ECLI:EU:C:2013:275. The ECJ held that statements by the 'patron' of a professional football club that he would never hire a homosexual player may shift the burden of proof on to the club to prove that it does not have a discriminatory recruitment policy, and that the Romanian remedy of only a warning for such conduct could not be *seen* as effective, proportionate and dissuasive under the requirements of Directive 2000/78/EC.

63 Case C-83/14 *CHEZ Razpredelenie Bulgaria AD v. Komisia za zashtita ot diskriminatsia* [2015] ECLI:EU:C:2015:480 . In this case, the Court found a Bulgarian electricity company conducted "offensive and stigmatizing" practices that violate European antidiscrimination laws by placing electrical meters at a height of 7 meters in a Roma residential area. The plaintiff in the case was not Roma but lived in the neighborhood.

prohibiting the visible wearing of any political, philosophical or religious signs. This holding is somewhat nuanced in the companion case, where the Court found that in the absence of such a rule, the willingness of an employer to take into account customer preferences as to discontinuing the employer's services due to employees wearing Islamic headscarves cannot be considered an occupational requirement that can negate discrimination.[64]

## Part 3: Regional Human Rights Instruments and Discrimination Protections

Five regional cooperations outside of Europe have adopted human rights instruments: the Organization of American States, the African Union, the Organisation of Islamic Cooperation, the League of Arab States and the Commonwealth of Independent States comprising former Soviet states, presented in this order below. There is no regional cooperation in Asia with respect to human rights, but two non-governmental organizations, the Asian Human Rights Commission[65] and the Asian Legal Resource Centre, work with raising consciousness as to human rights in Asia. The latter has General Consultative Status with the United Nations Economic and Social Council. Each of the regional cooperations discussed below have promulgated human rights instruments that are in response to the UN documents discussed in the previous part and also incoporporating all three generations of human rights. As with the international legal instruments, explicit protections against discrimination on the basis of age or LGBTQUIA issues are absent in many of the regional discrimination instruments. This is not surprising as these regional instruments are fairly faithful to the UN structures, demonstrating the significance of the international documents on the regional levels.

### *The Organization of American States*

The Organization of American States ("OAS") claims the title of the world's oldest regional organization, dating its foundation back to the First International Conference of American States held in Washington, D.C. from 1889–1890. The 1948 OAS Charter was originally signed by twenty-one American countries and

64 Cases C-157/15 *Achbita, Centrum voor Gelijkheid van kansen en voor racismebestrijding v. G4S Secure Solutions*, [2017] ECLI:EU:C:2017:203 and C-188/15 *Bougnaoui and Association de défense des droits de l'homme (ADDH) v. Micropole Univers* [2017] ECLI:EU:C:2017:204.

65 For more information on the Asian Human Rights Commission, *see* its website, humanrights.asia, and on the Asian Legal Resource Centre, its website, alrc.asia.

today, all thirty-five independent states of the Americas are OAS members and have ratified the Charter.[66] The Charter addresses issues of social justice and the fundamental rights of individuals without distinction as to race, nationality, creed or sex.

The American Declaration of the Rights and Duties of Man was also adopted at the 1948 conference. The Declaration begins by affirming that "[a]ll men are born free and equal, in dignity and in rights, and, being endowed by nature with reason and conscience, they should conduct themselves as brothers one to another." The Declaration lists both rights and duties, stating in its preamble that the "fulfillment of duty by each individual is a prerequisite to the rights of all. Rights and duties are interrelated in every social and political activity of man. While rights exalt individual liberty, duties express the dignity of that liberty." Rights include equality before the law "without distinction as to race, sex, language, creed or any other factor." Duties include to society, children and families, to becoming educated, paying taxes, voting, obeying the law and working. That same year, Inter-American conventions were adopted on granting political and civil rights to women. The Inter-American Commission on Human Rights ("IACHR") was created in 1959 to supervise the enforcement of these instruments,[67] with the Inter-American Court of Human Rights created later in 1979.[68]

The OAS Charter was amended significantly by a 1967 protocol with a greater emphasis on social justice. Its revised Article 31 includes in its goals fair wages, employment opportunities, acceptable working conditions, the rapid eradication of illiteracy and the expansion of educational opportunities for all. The revised Article 43 states that "[a]ll human beings, without distinction as to race, sex, nationality, creed, or social condition, have a right to material well-being and to their spiritual development, under circumstances of liberty, dignity, equality of opportunity, and economic security." Access to justice is also raised by providing "[a]dequate provision for all persons to have due legal aid in order to secure their rights."

66 The OAS member states are: Antigua and Barbuda, Argentina, Bahamas, Barbados, Belize, Bolivia, Brazil, Canada, Colombia, Costa Rica, Chile, Dominica, Dominican Republic, Ecuador, El Salvador, Grenada, Guatemala, Guyana, Haiti, Honduras, Jamaica, Mexico, Nicaragua, Panama, Paraguay, Peru, Saint Kitts and Nevis, Saint Lucia, Saint Vicente and the Grenadines, Suriname, Trinidad and Tobago, United States of America, Uruguay, and Venezuela. For more information on the OAS *see* its website, oas.org.

67 For more information on the IACHR, and its merit reports on cases, *see* its website, oas.org/en/iachr.

68 For more information on the Court, as well as its judgments and caseload, *see* its website at corteidh.or.cr.

The American Convention on Human Rights opened for signatures in 1969 and came into force in 1978, with twenty-five nations having signed it to date. The Convention begins with the general obligation for all States Parties to ensure that persons within their jurisdiction have the free and full exercise of those rights and freedoms under the Convention, "without any discrimination for reasons of race, color, sex, language, religion, political or other opinion, national or social origin, economic status, birth, or any other social condition."

The Convention is structured in two parts, civil and political rights (articles 3–25), and economic, social and cultural rights (Article 26), mirroring the structure of the UN ICCPR and ICESCR. Under the civil and political rights, article 3 states that every person, defined in the convention as every human being, has the "right to recognition as a person before the law." Freedom from slavery is protected under Article 6 in that slavery, involuntary servitude, forced and compulsory labor, the slave trade and trafficking in women are prohibited. The rights to life from inception, personal liberty, fair trials, due process, privacy, nationality, property, family, name, government participation, freedom of conscience, religion, thought, expression, assembly, association, movement and residence, protection from inhumane treatment including respect of an individual's physical, mental and moral integrity, the right of reply to defamatory statements, and the rights of the child are included in this first part. Article 26 as to economic, social, and cultural rights states that the standards articulated in the OAS Charter and its 1967 Protocol of Amendment are to be upheld.

Duties and personal responsibilities, including the relationship between duties and rights, are set out in Article 32. Every person "has responsibilities to his family, his community, and mankind" and that the "rights of each person are limited by the rights of others, by the security of all, and by the just demands of the general welfare, in a democratic society." The Convention also establishes the Inter-American Court of Human Rights, which then was created in 1979 when the Convention entered into force.

The OAS has also adopted several conventions addressing specific topics of discrimination: granting political[69] and civil rights to women,[70] the prevention, punishment and eradication of violence against women,[71] the elimination of all forms of discrimination against persons with disabilities,[72] and

69 1948 Inter-American Convention on the Granting of Political Rights to Women (A-44).

70 1948 Inter-American Convention on the Granting of Civil Rights to Women (A-45).

71 2013 Inter-American Convention Against Racism, Racial Discrimination and Related Forms of Intolerance (A-68).

72 1999 Inter-American Convention on the Elimination of All Forms of Discrimination Against Persons with Disabilities.

the protection of the human rights of older persons.[73] The Inter-American Convention Against All Forms of Discrimination and Intolerance calls for the eradication of all discrimination based on nationality, age, sex, sexual orientation, gender identity and expression, language, religion, cultural identity, political opinions or opinions of any kind, social origin, socioeconomic status, educational level, migrant, refugee, repatriate, stateless or internally displaced status, disability, genetic trait, mental or physical health condition, including infectious-contagious condition and debilitating psychological condition, or any other condition.[74]

A Social Charter of the Americas was adopted in 2012, with its Article 1 stating that the "peoples of the Americas legitimately aspire to social justice and their governments have a responsibility to promote it." To achieve social justice, development with equity is to strengthen and consolidate democracy, within a framework of solidarity, equity, peace, and freedom. Poverty is to be eliminated, especially extreme poverty, with a decent standard of living for all. The Member states reaffirm their commitment to universal respect for and observance of human rights and fundamental freedoms as essential elements to achieve social justice and strengthen democracy, as everyone is born free and equal in dignity and rights.

Article 3 mandates that the Member States assume the responsibility "for achieving development with social justice for their peoples, thus contributing to strengthening democratic governance." The Member States are also to "develop and implement comprehensive social protection policies and programs, based on the principles of universality, solidarity, equality, non-discrimination, and equity that give priority to persons living in conditions of poverty and vulnerability, taking into account their national circumstances" as set out in Article 14.

The enforcement of these instruments rests upon both monitoring and complaint procedures. Individuals or organizations can file complaints to the IACHR as to violations of those human rights recognized in the American Convention on Human Rights. If the IACHR finds the petition admissible, it is forwarded to the state involved for a response. The Commission tries to reach settlements between the parties respecting the human rights. If a settlement is not reached, the case can be forwarded to the Court,[75] for example sixteen

73 2015 Inter-American Convention on Protecting the Human Rights of Older Persons (A-70).

74 2013 Inter-American Convention Against All Forms of Discrimination and Intolerance (A-69).

75 Twenty-one States Parties have acknowledged the Court's jurisdiction in such matters: Costa Rica, Peru, Venezuela, Honduras, Ecuador, Argentina, Uruguay, Colombia, Guatemala,

cases were referred to the Court in 2016.[76] Judgments of the Court in 2016 addressed topics such as slavery and human-trafficking, informed consent for medical female sterilization, prohibiting discrimination against same-sex couples in relation to patrimonial rights, procedural guarantees, forced displacements, enforced disappearances, and the rights of indigenous peoples.[77]

### *The African Union*

The Organisation of African Unity ("OAU") was founded in 1963 comprising thirty-two African governments. The OAU had the aim of coordinating and intensifying the cooperation of African states in order to achieve better lives, ensure human rights, and raise the standard of living for all Africans. There was no explicit obligation for member states to protect human rights under the OAU Charter initially, only to have due regard for the human rights as set out in the UNDHR. The OAU was replaced in 2002 by the African Union ("AU").[78] The objectives of the AU include promoting human and peoples' rights in accordance with the 1981 African (Banjul) Charter on Human and Peoples' Rights and other relevant human rights instruments. All fifty-three AU members are parties to the Charter. The States Parties affirm in its preamble that they are:

> Conscious of their duty to achieve the total liberation of Africa, the peoples of which are still struggling for their dignity and genuine independence, and undertaking to eliminate colonialism, neo-colonialism, apartheid, zionism and to dismantle aggressive foreign military bases and all forms of discrimination, particularly those based on race, ethnic group, color, sex, language, religion or political opinions …

Every individual is entitled under Article 2 to the "enjoyment of the rights and freedoms recognized and guaranteed in the present Charter without distinction of any kind such as race, ethnic group, color, sex, language, religion, political or any other opinion, national and social origin, fortune, birth or other status."

---

Suriname, Panama, Chile, Nicaragua, Paraguay, Bolivia, El Salvador, Haiti, Brazil, Mexico, Dominican Republic, and Barbados. For more information on information on the Inter-American Court of Human Rights, *see* its website, corteidh.or.cr.

76 *See* OAS, ANNUAL REPORT OF THE GENERAL SECRETARY (2016), available at the OAS website, oas.org. under the headings documents, then annual reports.

77 *See* the Inter-American Court of Human Rights, ANNUAL REPORT (2016) available at its website, corteidh.or.cr, under the headings.

78 For more information on the African Union, *see* its website, au.int.

The Charter recognizes the indivisibility of all rights, and contains no derogation clauses. It sets out both rights and duties. Every individual is to be equal before the law, and entitled to the equal protection of the law, respect for life and to dignity. All forms of exploitation and degradation, particularly "slavery, the slave trade, torture, cruel, inhumane or degrading punishment and treatment" are prohibited (Article 5). The rights protected are to liberty, security of person, due process, information, public service, public property, property, health, education, culture and tradition, family, economic, social and cultural developments, enjoyment of the common heritage of mankind, development, national and international peace and security, and a generally satisfactory environment. Freedoms of conscience, profession, religion, expression, association, assembly, movement and political participation are also protected. Equal pay for equal work (Article 15) and the elimination of every discrimination against women, special protection of the rights of women, children and the elderly (Article 18) are explicitly mentioned. Article 19 mandates that all "peoples shall be equal; they shall enjoy the same respect and shall have the same rights. Nothing shall justify the domination of a people by another."

The duties prescribed under the African Charter include to the family, society and state, to respect and consider fellow beings without discrimination, maintain mutual respect and tolerance, as well as under Article 29 to:

1. Preserve the harmonious development of the family and to work for the cohesion and respect of the family, to respect his parents at all times, to maintain them in case of need;
2. Serve his national community by placing his physical and intellectual abilities at its service;
3. Not compromise the security of the State whose national or resident he is;
4. Preserve and strengthen social and national solidarity, particularly when the latter is threatened;
5. Preserve and strengthen the national independence and the territorial integrity of his country and to contribute to its defense in accordance with the law;
6. Work to the best of his abilities and competence, and to pay taxes imposed by law in the interest of the society;
7. Preserve and strengthen positive African cultural values in his relations with other members of the society, in the spirit of tolerance, dialogue and consultation and, in general, to contribute to the promotion of the moral well being of society; and
8. Contribute to the best of his abilities, at all times and at all levels, to the promotion and achievement of African unity.

Other AU human rights documents that have been adopted include the 1990 African Charter on the Rights and Welfare of the Child and the 2003 Protocol to the African Charter on Human and Peoples' Rights on the Rights of Women in Africa ("Women's Protocol"). The Women's protocal addresses women's civil and political, economic, social and cultural, group, as well as health and reproductive rights. It calls for the elimination of all forms of discrimination against women. This is to be achieved by including in the States Parties' constitutions the principle of equality between women and men and ensuring its effective application, as well as legislating any necessary laws to reach that effect, and mainstreaming gender in all policy and legal decisions. The protocol also calls for national legislation prohibiting female genital mutilation. Women are to have access to justice and equal protection before the law. Rights to be granted to women include to dignity, life, integrity, security of person, voluntary marriage, separation, divorce, annulment of marriage, political participation, peace, education, training, economic and social welfare rights, health and reproductive rights, food security, adequate housing, positive cultural context, healthy and sustainable environment, sustainable development, widow's right, inheritance, with special protection of elderly women, women with disabilities and women in distress.

The African Commission on Human and Peoples' Rights[79] was created to promote and ensure the human and peoples' rights granted by the Charter through both reporting and complaints. The Commission receives complaints in the form of communications as to human rights violations from states, individuals or NGOs. Communications can be submitted by parties other than the victim. All domestic remedies are to be exhausted before filing a communication, with certain exceptions, such as indigence, massive violations, physical danger or where such a requirement is illogical. The Commission can provide legal aid if assessed as needed. By 2011 over 400 individual communications had been received.[80] If the Commission finds the communication admissible, the parties are requested to send their responses. If a settlement cannot be reached, the Commission decides the case on its merits.[81]

---

79 For more information on the African Commission on Human and Peoples' Rights and its decisions on communications, *see* its website at achpr.org.

80 *See* African Commission on Human and Peoples' Rights, CELEBRATING THE AFRICAN CHARTER AT 20: A GUIDE TO THE AFRICAN HUMAN RIGHTS SYSTEM (Pretoria Press 2011).

81 *See* the *41st Activity Report of the African Commission on Human and Peoples' Rights 2016, submitted in Accordance with Article 54 of the African Charter on Human and Peoples' Rights*, available at the Commission's website, achpr.org.

The pan-African Court on Human and Peoples' Rights[82] is also established under the AU Charter and to date, only eight countries have recognized its competence. The African Commission of Human and Peoples' Rights, State parties to the Protocol and African Intergovernmental Organizations have standing to file cases with the Court. NGOs with observer status before the African Commission and individuals can also institute cases directly before the Court as long as the state against which they are complaining has deposited the Article 34(6) declaration recognizing the jurisdiction of the Court to accept cases from individuals and NGOs. The Court delivered its first judgment in 2009. In its most recent judgment as of the date of this writing, the Court held that Kenya had violated several articles of the African Charter with respect to the Ogiek Community of the Mau Forest in October 2009. A 30-day eviction notice had been issued by the Kenya Forestry Service to the Ogieks and other settlers of the Mau Forest, demanding that they leave the forest without any procedural guarantees, appeal process or remedies. Kenya was ordered by the Court to take all appropriate measures within a reasonable time frame to remedy all the violations established and to inform the Court within six months of the measures taken.[83]

### *Organisation of Islamic Cooperation*

The Organisation of Islamic Conference was founded in 1969 by thirty member states, with its first Charter adopted in 1972 and the Cairo Declaration on Human Rights in Islam adopted in 1990. The association changed its name to the Organisation of Islamic Cooperation ("OIC") in 2011. The OIC presently consists of 57 member states, stating its mission as being the collective voice of the Muslim world.[84] The Cairo Declaration is a guide for member states as to human rights in Islam, clearly framed within Islamic Shari'ah, as seen from Articles 24 and 25 stating that all the "rights and freedoms stipulated in this Declaration are subject to the Islamic Shari'ah," and that the "Islamic Shari'ah is the only source of reference for the explanation or clarification of any of the articles of this Declaration." The Declaration's first article sets out a principle of non-discrimination:

82 For more information on the African Court on Human and Peoples' Rights and its judgments *see* its website, african-court.org.

83 Case, *African Commission on Human and Peoples' Rights v. Republic of Kenya*, application no. 006/2012.

84 For more information about the OIC, *see* its website, oic-oci.org.

(a) All human beings form one family whose members are united by their subordination to Allah and descent from Adam. All men are equal in terms of basic human dignity and basic obligations and responsibilities, without any discrimination on the basis of race, colour, language, belief, sex, religion, political affiliation, social status or other considerations. The true religion is the guarantee for enhancing such dignity along the path to human integrity.

(b) All human beings are Allah's subjects, and the most loved by Him are those who are most beneficial to His subjects, and no one has superiority over another except on the basis of piety and good deeds.

Article 19 prescribes that all individuals are equal before the law, without distinction between the ruler and the ruled, and that the right to resort to justice is guaranteed to everyone.

Slavery is forbidden under Article 11, as "[h]uman beings are born free, and no one has the right to enslave, humiliate, oppress or exploit them, and there can be no subjugation but to Allah the Almighty." Both men and women are entitled to fair wages without delay, leisure and promotion under Article 13. Women are specifically protected under Article 6, with a woman equal to a man "in human dignity, and having her own rights to enjoy as well as duties to perform, and her own civil entity and financial independence, and the right to retain her name and lineage."

The rights granted under the Declaration cover a broad spectrum of issues: the rights to life, safety from bodily harm, medical treatment, protection of name and body, marriage and family, education (both secular and religious), legal capacity, work, property, compensation for lawful expropriation, copyrights, patents, living in a pure environment, medical and social care, privacy, security, due process, information, freedoms of movement, residence, expression, political participation, internal family obligations between generations, with prohibitions as to genocide, killing civilians, destroying civilian property, usury and taking hostages.

The OIC has adopted a 2004 Covenant on the Rights of the Child in Islam and an OIC 2008 Plan of Action for the Advancement of Women, including the goal of eventually adopting a Covenant on the Rights of Women in Islam. The objectives of the action plan include the eradication of poverty, raising women's participation in public decision-making, providing equal opportunities for women through access to quality education, health-care and enhanced participation, and eliminating all forms of discrimination including combating violence against women.

The Independent Permanent Human Rights Commission came into being in 2011 with the mandate to monitor human rights within the OIC member states. Its tasks are informational and advisory.[85]

### *The League of Arab States*

The League of Arab States was created in 1945 with the adoption of the Charter of the League of Arab States by the governments of Syria, Transjordan, Iraq, Saudi Arabia, Lebanon, Egypt and North Yemen, a few months prior to the adoption of the UN Charter. Today there are twenty-one active country members in the League.[86] The Permanent Arab Commission on Human Rights was established in 1968, and a drafting process for an Arab charter on human rights began in 1969. A 1994 Arab Charter on Human Rights was drafted but never entered into force. The Arab Commission on Human Rights recommended revision, and the 2004 revised Charter came into force in 2008 upon its seventh ratification.[87]

The preamble to the Charter addresses several themes, commencing with the "Arab nation's belief in human dignity since God honoured it by making the Arab World the cradle of religions and the birthplace of civilizations which confirmed its right to a life of dignity based on freedom, justice and peace." The Charter affirms that "all human rights are universal, indivisible, interdependent and interrelated" citing the principles of the UN Charter, UNDHR, ICCPR and ICESCR, as well as the Cairo Declaration on Human Rights in Islam. The interpretation and application of the 2008 Charter is to be according to Islamic Shari'ah.

The rights under the Charter include the rights to self-determination, control over natural wealth and resources, freely determine the form of the political structure, and freely pursue economic, social and cultural development (Article 1).[88] Racism, Zionism, occupation and foreign domination are termed challenges to human dignity and constitute fundamental obstacles to the

---

85 For more information on the Commission, *see* its website, oic-iphrc.org.

86 The twenty-one active members are Algeria, Bahrain, Comoros, Djibouti, Egypt, Iraq, Jordan, Kuwait, Lebanon, Libya, Mauritania, Morocco, Oman, Palestine, Qatar, Saudi Arabia, Somalia, Sudan, Tunisia, United Arab Emirates and Yemen.

87 *See* Wail Allam, *The Arab Charter on Human Rights: Main Features*, 28 ARAB LAW QUARTERLY 40–63 (2014) and Mervat Rishmawi, *The Arab Charter on Human Rights and the League of Arab States: An Update*, 10:1 HUMAN RIGHTS L. REV. 169–178 (2010).

88 This English translation of the Charter is available at the website of the Swedish Human Rights Foundation, humanrights.se.

realization of the basic rights of peoples, with the articulated need to condemn and endeavor to eliminate such practices.

Each State Party is to ensure that all individuals within its territory and subject to its jurisdiction enjoy all the rights and freedoms recognized therein, without any distinction on the grounds of race, color, sex, language, religion, political opinion, national or social origin, property, birth or physical or mental disability, with an inherent right to recognition as a person before the law. The rights of women are taken up in several articles. Equal remuneration is to be paid to women and men for work of equal value. Under Article 3(3), "[m]en and women are equal in respect of human dignity, rights and obligations within the framework of the positive discrimination established in favour of women by the Islamic Shari'a, other divine laws and by applicable laws and legal instruments." Prostitution, sexual exploitation and the exploitation of the prostitution of others are prohibited under Article 10(2), as well as all forms of violence or abuse against women under Article 33(2). The right of every worker to enjoy just and favorable conditions in the workplace which ensures the protection of women are set out in Article 34(2). Article 41(3) emphasizes the effective participation of women in the field of development, with the State Parties having an obligation to take appropriate measures in all domains to ensure partnerships between men and women in achieving national development. Last, Article 43 prescribes that the Charter may not be construed or interpreted as impairing the rights of women.

Individuals with disabilities and minorities are also granted rights under the Charter. Discrimination on the grounds of "physical or mental disability" is prohibited under Article 33(2), state and society must "ensure the necessary protection and care for persons with special needs". State Parties are under an obligation according to Article 40 to ensure a decent life that guarantees the dignity of persons with mental or physical disabilities. Article 25 provides that individuals belonging to minorities are not to be denied the right to enjoy their own culture, use their own language and practice their own religion. Article 43 mandates that nothing in the Charter may be construed or interpreted as impairing the rights of persons belonging to minorities. The Charter also contains provisions with respect to the care of children and the elderly.

Rights to life, liberty, security of person, due process, presumption of innocence, privacy, political participation, freedom of movement and residence, political asylum, private property, trade unions and the taking of industrial actions, a basic standard of living, free choice of work, access to public office, adequate food, water, a healthy environment, freedoms with only lawful restrictions as to movement, residence, belief, thought, opinion, religion, peaceful assembly, and association, restrictions as to the use of capital punishment, prohibitions against inhumane treatment, imprisonment for debt, double jeopardy, are all set out in the Charter. Certain rights are granted only to citizens, such as the rights to work, free basic health care and free education.

The eradication of illiteracy is prescribed in Article 34 as a binding obligation, with every citizen having a right to education. Primary education is to be compulsory and free, and both secondary and university education are to be easily accessible to all. The right of citizens to live in an intellectual and cultural environment in which Arab nationalism is a source of pride is taken up in Article 35. Human rights are sanctified and racial, religious and other forms of discrimination are rejected and international cooperation and the cause of world peace are supported. Everyone is to have the right under Article 36 to participate in cultural life, as well as the right to enjoy literary and artistic works and to be given opportunities to develop his artistic, intellectual and creative talents.

A Committee of Experts on Human Rights is created under the Charter to receive Charter reports from the States Parties. The Committee is then to report to the Permanent Arab Commission on Human Rights at the Arab League. No individual complaint mechanism is available.

### *The Commonwealth of Independent States*

The Commonwealth of Independent States ("CIS") is a confederation formed in 1991 under the Belavzha Accords. Today it has nine member states, Armenia, Azerbaijan, Belarus, Kazakhstan, Kyrgyzstan, Moldova, Russia, Tajikistan, Uzbekistan, and two associate states, Turkmenistan and the Ukraine.[89] Georgia withdrew its membership in 2008. Its 1995 Convention on Human Rights and Fundamental Freedoms was drafted[90] to protect and prevent violations of human rights and fundamental freedoms irrespective of "race, sex, language, political beliefs, religion and social origin". Slavery, servitude, forced and compulsory labor are prohibited by Article 4. An interesting exception to forced labor concerns parental duties to children, and a child's duties to vulnerable

89 For more information on CIS *see* its website, cis.minsk.by.

90 Only four states have ratified the Convention, Russia, Belarus, Tajikistan, and Kyrgyzstan. The COE Parliament recommended in 2001 that those COE member-states that are also the CIS members, Armenia, Azerbaijan, Moldova, Russia, and Ukraine, not sign the CIS Convention on Human Rights, as the CIS Charter offered less protection than the ECHR, "both with regards to the scope of its contents, and with regard to the body enforcing it," *see* COE Parliamentary Assembly Resolution 1249 (2001), Co-existence of the Convention on Human Rights and Fundamental Freedoms of the Commonwealth of Independent States and the European Convention on Human Rights.

parents. Equal remuneration for equal work, maternal leave, illegality of any notice of employment dismissal during an absence on maternity leave, leave for nursing, the regulation of women's night work and underground mining work are all contained in the Convention. Persons with disabilities are to have the right to occupational rehabilitation, vocational training and social reintegration facilities (Art 18).

All are to be equal before the law and entitled without any discrimination to equal protection of the law (Article 20). The enjoyment of the rights and freedoms in the Convention are to be guaranteed without discrimination on any ground such as sex, race, color, language, religion, political or other opinion, national or social origin, association with a national minority, property or official capacity, place of birth or other status.

The rights granted in the Convention include to life, liberty and security of person, due process, public judicial decisions, presumption of innocence, information in a familiar language if arrested, compensation for unlawful detentions, appeals, private and family life, correspondence, legal and social protections for family life, the social and economic protection of mothers and children to work and protection from unemployment, to marry and have a family, citizenship, property ownership, education, vocational training, political participation, freedoms of thought, conscience and faith, of expression, peaceful assembly, association, movement, restrictions as to the death penalty, inhumane treatment, post facto laws, double jeopardy and expulsion. Children are to have the right to social protective measures from family, society and the State (Article 17). National minorities are not to be denied the rights, either individually or collectively, to express, preserve and developing, without hindrance, their ethnic, linguistic, cultural or religious identities (Article 21).

The Convention also establishes a Human Rights Commission of the Commonwealth of Independent States to monitor the execution of the Convention by the member states. The CIS Commission is to have the authority to examine individual applications by persons concerning alleged violations of the CIS Convention by member states.[91] The CIS Commission however has yet to become operational.

91 *See* Alastair Mowbry, CASES AND MATERIALS ON THE EUROPEAN CONVENTION ON HUMAN RIGHTS 888–9 (2004).

## Part 4: National Discrimination Legal Frameworks —The United States

Slavery forced both the American colonies initially, and the United States later as a country, to grapple with issues of labor and human rights. As early as the 1600's, New Amsterdam (later New York) passed laws outlawing slavery but still had a bifurcated labor force, with menial labor the province of former slaves and colonists of African descent. Labor issues became intimately intertwined with the question of independence from England as high taxes pushed down wages. A group of artisans and workers, The Sons of Liberty, began protesting English taxes in 1765. An auxiliary women's group, The Daughters of Liberty, became the first organization of working women, producing substitutes for the boycotted English goods as part of their patriotic duty.

Litigation concerning the legal status of slaves brought to Massachusetts began already by the 1780's, with courts finding the slaves to be free under the wording of the Massachusetts Constitution that "all men are born free and equal."[92] The issue of slavery could not be resolved by the drafters of the 1789 US Federal Constitution, with prrovisions favorable to slavery included in order to get it ratified: Slaves counted as three-fifths of a person for the apportionment of representatives and taxes (Article I, Section 2), Congress had no power to ban slavery until 1808 (Article I, Section 9), runaway slaves could not be protected in free states but had to be returned to their owners (Article IV, Section 2), and that no constitutional amendment banning slavery could be made until 1808 (Article V). The United States banned international slave trade and import in 1808, but continued to permit the ownership and sale of slaves domestically.

The rights of Native Americans were also restricted by law. Under the European doctrine of "discovery", European powers first discovering a land not inhabited by Christian Europeans could claim that territory as their own. Native rights to the land remained, but the land could then only be sold to the European country that discovered it. Recognizing Native Americans as sovereign peoples, allowed first the English, then Americans, to legally restrict their rights through laws and contracts, with disease and war decimating their populations. Congress was given the exclusive power under the Constitution to regulate commerce with foreign nations, and among the several states, and with the Indian Tribes. Federal legislation was passed in 1790 prohibiting states and individuals from dealing with the tribes and buying land.

---

92 *Brom and Bet v. Ashley* (Berkshire County Court of Common Pleas Massachusetts 1781) and *Quock Wallker v. Jennison* (Worcester County Court of Common Pleas Massachusetts 1781).

Discussions as to the rights of women were also present in the colonial period. Despite Abigail Adam's admonition to her husband to "remember the ladies" when drafting the Constitution, it was not until 1919 that the Constitution was amended to give women the right to vote. The first all-female strike demanding a wage increase was conducted by the United Tailoresses of New York in 1825. The movement for women's equality and suffrage joined efforts with the abolitionist anti-slavery movement already by the 1830's. The Lowell Female Labor Reform Association was founded in 1844 as one of the first American labor groups organized by and for women.[93] The Typographers Union was founded in 1856 and women were admitted as members beginning in 1869.[94] The first significant central labor organization was the Knights of Labor, founded among garment cutters in 1869 in Philadelphia, dedicated to organizing all workers for their general welfare. It was one of the first to work for organizing women nationally, appointing Leonora Barry in 1887 to this task. By 1886, the Knights had about 700 000 members, including African-Americans, women, wage earners, merchants and farmers.[95] The path of women in the labor unions, however, was not always straight nor always positive, with backlashes of male resistance to women's rights and employment often occurring.

The US Supreme Court held in *Dred Scott v. Sanford* (1857) that individuals of African descent could never be citizens of the United States as their ancestors had been slaves. Chief Justice Taney distinguished African-Americans from Native Americans, stating that "although they were uncivilized, [Native Americans] were yet a free and independent people, associated together in nations or tribes and governed by their own laws" and consequently could become citizens.[96] The Civil War followed closely on the heels of this decision, and after 600,000 casualties, the United States prevailed over the Confederacy in 1865. Three federal civil rights amendments were passed, the 13th Amendment (1865) banning slavery and involuntary servitude, the 14th Amendment (1868) defining American citizenship and its rights, as well as equal rights to due

93 By the 1860's, the Lowell mills employed over 60 000 female workers, *see* Robert Belton, Dianne Avery, EMPLOYMENT LAW DISCRIMINATION, CASES AND MATERIALS ON EQUALITY IN THE WORKPLACE 343 (6th ed. West 1999).

94 The Typographers Union is the oldest American labor union that is still active, *see* The Printing, Publishing and Media Workers Sector of the Communication Workers of America website, cwa-ppmws.org.

95 *See* Joseph Golowka, "There shall be no sex in industry": Women and gender in the Knights of Labor of North America, 1878–1893 (ProQuest 2013).

96 *Dred Scott v. Sandford*, 60 U.S. 393, 403 (1857). The Court erred procedurally, as by finding Dred Scott not to be a citizen, he then had no standing to bring the lawsuit and the case should have been dismissed on procedural grounds instead of addressed on its merits.

process, life, liberty and property, and the 15th Amendment (1870) prohibiting the denial of American [male] citizens the right to vote based on race, color or past servitude. The Federal Civil Rights Act of 1866, the first in a line of civil rights acts, guaranteed the rights of all citizens to make and enforce contracts, and to purchase, sell, or lease property.[97] Despite the constitutional amendments and several Civil Rights Acts, certain states began to build a system of apartheid with Jim Crow laws, establishing separate schools, medical facilities, public accommodations, housing, transportation, movie theatres, hotels and even drinking fountains for blacks and whites. This system was condoned by the US Supreme Court in *Plessy v. Ferguson* in 1896 with the Court holding that nominally separate but equal transportation facilities were not a badge of inferiority and not in violation of either the 13th or 14th Amendments.[98]

With respect to workers, the federal government prohibited unequal wages between men and women in federal service in 1870 due to the participation of women in employment during the civil war. Protective legislation was passed at both the federal and state levels concerning work day limits for all workers (a result of the 10-hour campaign), restricting the employment of children and women, and setting wages in certain industries. The latter stemmed partly from a true desire to protect, but also in response to the perceived threat against

97 This 1866 Civil Rights Act was the first in a series of civil rights acts enacted in 1870, 1871, 1875, 1957 and 1960: First Ku Klux Klan Act (Civil Rights Act of 1870) (prohibited discrimination in voter registration on the basis of race, color, or previous condition of servitude and established penalties for interfering with a person's right to vote, giving federal courts the power to enforce the act and to employ the use of federal marshals and the army to uphold it); Second Ku Klux Klan Act (Civil Rights Act of 1871) (All elections in both the North and South placed under federal control); Third Ku Klux Klan Act (1871) (enforces the 14th Amendment by guaranteeing all citizens of the United States the rights afforded by the Constitution and provided legal protection under the law); Civil Rights Act of 1875 (bars discrimination in public accommodations and on public conveyances on land and water, and prohibits the exclusion of African-Americans from jury duty); Civil Rights Act of 1957 (created the Commission on Civil Rights and the Civil Rights Division in the U.S. Department of Justice, authorizing the U.S. Attorney General to seek court injunctions against deprivation and obstruction of voting rights by state officials); and Civil Rights Act of 1960 (expanding the enforcement powers of the Civil Rights Act of 1957, introducing criminal penalties for obstructing the implementation of federal court orders and requiring that voting and registration records for federal elections be preserved).

98 Justice Harlan dissenting, stating that "[i]n my opinion, the judgment this day rendered will, in time, prove to be quite as pernicious as the decision made by this tribunal in the Dred Scott Case," *see Plessy v. Ferguson*, 163 U.S. 537, 559 (1896).

male workers.[99] Considerable protective legislation had been passed by the 1900's as to the work of children, women, wage and hours laws, as well as factory inspectors. Massachusetts adopted the first minimum wage for women and minors in 1912. The Court initially held that protective legislation with respect to children and women was not in violation of the American federal equal protection and due process clause of the 14th amendment if the legislation had a rational basis.[100] In contrast, the Court viewed general protective employment legislation as infringing the freedom of contract during its Lochner period.[101]

Congress passed the Railway Labor Act of 1926 requiring employers to bargain with unions and prohibiting discrimination on the basis of union membership. During the Great Depression in the 1930's the federal government was called upon to solve the significant problem of unemployment, which at its worst was one-third of the American workforce. Laws passed on the federal level included the Norris-LaGuardia Act (1932) prohibiting federal injunctions in labor disputes and outlawing anti-union employment contracts, the National Industrial Recovery Act guaranting the rights of employees to organize and bargain collectively (1933),[102] the National Labor Relations Act (1935) establishing the National Labor Relations Board, the Social Security Act (1935), and the Fair Labor Standards Act (1938) establishing a 40-hour work week nationally, a minimum wage as well as banning child labor for goods sold in interstate commerce. Congress also implemented unemployment programs and insurance, residential loan programs and publicly-funded housing. The Conservation Corps was created to provide jobs and "[t]hat in employing citizens for the purpose of this Act, no discrimination shall be made on account

99 Lawrence M. Friedman, A HISTORY OF AMERICAN LAW 561 (3rd ed. New York 2005). *See also* Alice Kessler-Harris, OUT TO WORK—A HISTORY OF WAGE-EARNING WOMEN IN THE UNITED STATES 180 (Oxford 2003) who notes a third reasoning, echoing from the early intergovernmental conferences, that it was viewed as easier to first pass such specific protective laws for women and children then move on to general laws for the entire labor force.

100 *See Muller v. Oregon*, 208 U.S. 412 (1908) in which the famous *Brandeis* brief was submitted, based predominantly on sociological evidence as to the detrimental effect of certain labor on the health of women.

101 *See, e.g., Lochner v. New York*, 198 U.S. 45 (1905)(New York law was not a constitutional regulation of workplace health and safety under state police power, violating freedom of contract as guaranteed by the 14th Amendment).

102 The Court declared this act unconstitutional in *A.L.A. Schechter Poultry Corp. v. United States*, 295 U.S. 495 (1935).

of race, color, or creed."[103] After initial resistance by the Court as to this exercise of legislative power in line with freedom of contract reasoning of *Lochner*, the Court acknowledged the constitutionality of these acts under Congress' powers as granted by the commerce clause in the infamous "switch in time that saved nine."[104]

Beginning in 1941 with President Roosevelt's Executive Order ("EO") 8802, executive orders have been issued prohibiting discrimination by private employers contracting with the federal government to perform work above a certain amount. EO 8802 prohibited discrimination on the basis of race, color, national origin or religion racial discrimination in the military defense industry as a response to a planned Washington march of over 100,000 individuals to protest such racial discrimination in the military. EO 8802 also established Fair Employment Practices ("FEP") Committees to investigate complaints of discrimination against such employers.[105] A duty of fair representation was imposed by the Court in the 1940's on labor unions to protect minority interests based on the 1926 Railway Labor Act and later the 1935 National Labor Relations Act. This duty of representation was imposed based on the union's status as the exclusive bargaining agent for all employees in the bargaining unit. This duty entails representing the interests of all of its members, minorities as well as the majority, organized as well as unorganized.

A minority group falling outside any pretense of discrimination protection was Asians. Anti-Chinese sentiment started with the California Gold Rush in the late 19th century during an influx of Chinese migrant laborers. AFL President Samuel Gompers published a pamphlet in 1901 entitled: "Meat vs. Rice: American Manhood v. Asiatic Coolieism, Which Shall Survive?" to argue for the extension of the 1882 Chinese Exclusion Act. With its extension in 1902, the Act barred all Chinese from naturalized American citizenship. Japanese were also targets of racism, with many states barring them from owning land, being naturalized as citizens or voting. This racism was taken to new heights during World War II. President Franklin Roosevelt signed EO 9066 ordering all Japanese-Americans in 1942 to evacuate the West coast during 1944–45, approximately 120,000 individuals, the majority of whom were American citizens. The

103 The 1933 Federal Act for the Relief of Unemployment Through the Performance of Useful Public Work, and for Other Purposes, 48 Stat. 22.

104 *See West Coast Hotel Co. v. Parrish*, 300 U.S. 379 (1937).

105 During the 1940's, approximately 24 states enacted FEP anti-discrimination legislation, *see* Anthony S. Chen, *The Hitlerian Rule of Quotas: Racial Conservatism and the Politics of Fair Employment Legislation in New York State, 1941–1945*, 92(4) THE J. OF AM. HISTORY 1238–1264 (2006).

Court upheld the legality of this relocation order despite the absence of any concrete evidence of espionage by Asian Americans.[106] Six year later, President Harry S. Truman issued EO 9981 mandating equality of treatment and opportunity in the armed services regardless of race, color, religion or national origin. Issues of racial discrimination, the legacy and badges of slavery, were brought to a head in the 1950's and 1960's. After decades of inaction by Congress, the Court finally in 1954 held in *Brown v. Board of Education* that the segregation of students based on race in public primary schools violates the Equal Protection Clause of the 14th Amendment as separate facilities are inherently unequal.[107]

### *The Federal Equal Pay Act of 1963*

The movement for equal pay legislation during the Civil War became a focus again by the need for female labor during World War I, with the Women's Bureau within the Department of Labor ("DOL") pressing for national legislation. The National War Labor Board worked for defense manufacturers to pay women at the same rate as men.[108] Congress enacted legislation in 1923 classifying positions and pay scales in the federal civil service, incorporating principles of merit and equal pay. However, the increase in female labor by six million workers during World War II finally provided the definitive momentum towards equal pay and equal rights. Feminist proponents had argued that "as we make progress in working against the Jim Crow laws of the nation, it is high time that we also work against the Jane Crow laws."[109] After almost two decades of annual introductions of equal pay bills to Congress, President Kennedy signed the Equal Pay Act of 1963 ("EPA")[110] into law as an amendment to the Fair Labor Standards Act. The objective of the EPA was to remedy what was perceived as "a serious and endemic problem of employment discrimination in private industry," the fact that the wage structure in many segments of American industry had "been based on an ancient but outmoded belief that a man, because of his role in society, should be paid more than a woman

106 *Hirabayashi v. United States*, 320 U.S. 81 (1943) and *Korematsu v. United States*, 323 U.S. 214 (1944). Congress in 1988 awarded restitution payments of $20,000.00 to each survivor of these camps, *see* Margaret Chon, *Remembering and Repairing: The Error Before Us, In Our Presence*, 8(2) SEA.J.SOC.JUS. 643 (2010).

107 *Brown v. Board of Education*, 387 U.S. 483 (1954).

108 *See* Elizabeth J. Wyman, *The Unenforced Promise of Equal Pay Acts: A National Problem and Possible Solution from Maine*, 55 ME L. REV. 23 (2003).

109 Kessler-Harris 242.

110 The Equal Pay Act, 29 U.S.C. § 206(d)(1).

even though his duties are the same."[111] At that time, full-time American working women were paid on average 59 cents to the dollar earned by their male counterparts.[112]

The EPA prohibits discrimination on the basis of sex in the payment of wages or benefits, where men and women perform work of substantially equal skill, effort, and responsibility, for the same employer under similar working conditions. It is unlawful for employers to reduce the wages of either sex to equalize pay.[113] Labor organizations, or their agents, representing employees of an employer subject to the EPA, are not to cause or attempt to cause employers to discriminate against employees in violation of the EPA's equal wage provisions.[114] The rules concerning equal pay are to "be liberally construed to effectuate the purpose and provisions of this Act and any other Act administered by the Commission issued by the Secretary of Labor."[115]

To prove a *prima facie* case under the EPA, the plaintiff must establish that: (i) in the same establishment, (ii) the employer pays different wages to employees of the opposite sex, (iii) who perform equal work on jobs requiring equal skill, effort and responsibility, and (iv) the jobs are performed under similar working conditions.[116] Discriminatory intent is not an element in an EPA case. Once plaintiff establishes a *prima facie* EPA violation, defendant bears both the burden of persuasion and production on its affirmative defenses.[117] Employers have record-keeping requirements of two years.[118] The Lilly Ledbetter Fair Pay Act of 2009 modified the statute of limitations for EPA claims, which no longer begin to toll with the first unequal paycheck, but instead with the last.[119] The statute of limitations for equal pay claims under the EPA is two years, unless a willful violation then three years. Charges can be filed with the Equal

111 *See Corning Glass Works v. Brennan*, 417 U.S. 188, 195 (1974) *citing* S.Rep. No. 176, 88th Cong., 1st Sess. 1 (1963).

112 *See* Warren Farrell, *Are Women Earning More Than Men?*, FORBES 12 May 2006.

113 *See* 29 C.F.R. § 1620.25. The simplicity of the EPA's language is somewhat illusory, as extensive regulations have been issued in conjunction with the EPA both as to substantive and procedural issues. As the EPA is part of the larger and more extensive Fair Labor Standards Act ("FLSA"), issues not specifically addressed within the wording of the EPA can fall within the broader FLSA. Wage discrimination claims on the basis other than sex can be made under Title VII.

114 The Equal Pay Act, 29 U.S.C. § 206(d)(2) and (3).

115 See 29 C.F.R. § 1620.34(a).

116 *See, e.g., Rhonda Tenkku v. Normandy Bank*, 348 F.3d 737, 741 (8th Cir. 2003).

117 *See Buntin v. Breathitt County Board of Education*, 134 F.3d 796, 800 (6th Cir. 1998).

118 *See* 29 C.F.R. § 1620.32, Recordkeeping Requirements.

119 Public Law 111–2, 123 Stat. 5 (2009).

Employment Opportunity Commission ("EEOC"), complains with the US Department of Labour, Wage and Hour Division, but plaintiffs can also directly litigate such claims.

The primary remedy available under the EPA is an award of damages in the form of backpay, the amount of the wages withheld in violation of the act.[120] The court is to determine whether the employer acted in good faith or willfully. An employer can show it acted in good faith if it had reasonable grounds for believing that the act or omission was not a violation of the federal Fair Labor Standards Act. If the employer is found to be in good faith, the employer then is only liable for back pay. If the employer's actions are found to be willful, back pay and an amount of liquidated damages equal to the back-pay award can be awarded.[121] An award of liquidated damages is mandatory in cases of willfulness. "Willful" is defined as more than negligence, where the employer "knew or showed reckless disregard as to whether its conduct was prohibited by statute."[122] A court may also order an injunction to restrain the employer from such future actions violating the law. Willful EPA violations can be criminally prosecuted, with fines up to $10 000 for a first violation, and six-months' imprisonment for a second.

During the period from 1960 to 2015, American women's real earnings increased 73%, from $21,646 (1960) to $37,388 (2015), while men's earnings increased by 27%, from $35,675 (1960) to $45,292 (2015). Women's median wages were 83% of men's median wages in 2015.[123] During the first ten years of EPA enforcement, a total of over $65 million in back pay was awarded.[124] For the ten-year period between 2006 to 2016, the EEOC recovered approximately $94.4 million in back pay.[125] In a recent 2014 settlement, plaintiffs argued that female school safety agents and male peace officers, both working in public buildings for the city of New York, should have the same pay and that the $7,000 a year gap was not lawful. The city settled for $145.5 million gross, $38 million for the

120 *See* 29 C.F.R. § 1620.33 (b) "Recovery of wages due; injunctions; penalties for willful violations".

121 29 U.S.C. § 216(b).

122 *See Trans World Airlines, Inc. v. Thurston*, 469 U.S. 111 (1985).

123 U.S. Bureau of Labor Statistics Reports, Women in the labor force: A databook (BLS Dec. 2015) available at bls.gov.

124 Barbara Babcock, SEX DISCRIMINATION AND THE LAW: CAUSES AND REMEDIES 440 (New York 1975).

125 *See* the EEOC Statistics Concerning "Equal Pay Charges" at the EEOC website, eeoc.gov.

class, $47 million to be spent raising salaries, and a new contract was entered into with Teamsters Local 237 with a 33% raise for 5,000 school safety agents.[126]

### *State Equal Pay Legislation*

Two states had passed legislation already by 1919 banning unequal pay by private employers, Michigan and Montana.[127] As of 2015, 48 states have equal pay acts.[128] Five states have equal wages for "same" or "comparable work" legislation. Over twenty states and municipalities have adopted comparable work legislation for public employers. Maine by way of example enacted an equal pay for equal work statute in 1949, amended it in 1965 to an equal pay for comparable worth statute, then strengthened its administrative procedures in 2001 with an administrative claims process and employers' self-auditing to encourage voluntary compliance.[129] Minnesota is another such example, with the State Employees Pay Equity Law also invoking the concept of comparable worth:[130]

> It is the policy of this state to attempt to establish equitable compensation relationships between female-dominated, male-dominated, and balanced classes of employees in the executive branch. Compensation relationships are equitable within the meaning of this subdivision when the primary consideration in negotiating, establishing, recommending, and approving total compensation is comparability of the value of the work in relationship to other positions in the executive branch.

---

126 *Mayor de Blasio and School Safety Agents Announce Tentative Contract Agreement, Proposed Settlement of Pay Equity Litigation* (August 2014) available at the City of New York website, nyc.gov. The Court's decision in *Wal-Mart Stores, Inc. v. Dukes* 564 U.S. 338 (2011) heightened the requirements for certifying a class, which in that case was claiming gender discrimination in pay and promotion policies.

127 *See* Kessler-Harris 234 (2001) and Belton 345(1999) 345.

128 *See* AAUW, 2015 State Equal Pay Legislation by Numbers (2015) available at its website, aauw.org. State or local equal pay provisions are specifically allowed to differ according to 29 C.F.R. § 1620.28 from the equal pay provisions set forth in the FLSA. However, "[n]o provisions of the EPA will excuse noncompliance with any State or other law establishing fewer defenses or more liberal work criteria than those of the EPA. On the other hand, compliance with other applicable legislation will not excuse violations of the EPA."

129 *See* Wyman at 25 *citing* Me. Dep't of Labor Reg. 12–170, Ch. 12 (Nov. 19, 2001).

130 Minn.Stat. § 43A.01-3, -14a, and -22a.

The pay equity system in Minnesota from its inception in 1983 to 2013 is estimated to have resulted in female state employees earning 89% of men's wages in 2014 in contrast to 69% in 1976.[131]

### *The Federal Civil Rights Act of 1964*

African-American children marched peacefully in protest as part of the desegregation campaign led by Dr. Martin Luther King Jr. in Birmingham, Alabama in May 1963. The children were met by the police with fire hoses and canine units with several thousand arrested. President Kennedy sent an emissary to broker a settlement, and ultimately by the end of the month, requested that the Department of Justice draft civil rights legislation.[132] Several months later, one quarter of a million demonstrators marched on Washington D.C. for jobs and freedom, listening to Dr. King's "I Have a Dream" speech. President Kennedy met with the march leaders to try to dissuade them from attempting to strengthen Title VII and other portions of the Civil Rights Bill, as he feared doing so would kill the needed Republican support. Two weeks later, several children were killed when an African-American church was bombed in Birmingham. Supporters of the Civil Rights Bill responded by strengthening key provisions, particularly the employment measures in Title VII. The bill was sent to the Rules Committee the day before President Kennedy was assassinated. Five days after the assassination, President Johnson addressed a joint session of Congress on 27 November 1963, stating:

> We have talked long enough in this country about civil rights. It is time to write the next chapter and to write it in the books of law ... No eulogy could more eloquently honor President Kennedy's memory than the earliest possible passage of the civil rights bill for which he fought so long.

The proposed bill did not initially include a prohibition as to discrimination on the basis of sex.[133] Debate exists as to the motives for its inclusion, with

131 Legislative Office on the Economic Status of Women, SUMMARY—PAY EQUITY: THE MINNESOTA EXPERIENCE (6th ed. 2016) available at its website, oesw.leg.mn.

132 *See* David B. Oppenheimer, *Kennedy, King, Shuttlesworth and Walker: The Events Leading to the Introduction of the Civil Rights Act of 1964*, 29 U. SAN FRANCISCO L. REV. 645 (1995). *See* the related Court cases, *Walker v. City of Birmingham*, 388 U.S. 307 (1967) and *Shuttlesworth v. City of Birmingham*, 394 U.S. 147 (1969).

133 The proposed federal Equal Rights Amendment ("ERA"), first introduced to Congress in 1923, has consistently failed to gather the ratifications necessary for a federal constitutional amendment.

some arguing that sex was added in an effort to defeat the bill. Women's rights groups had organized around the omission of "sex," arguing that the rights of African-American women were protected under the category of race while Caucasian women would continue to be disadvantaged because of their sex.[134] The proposal to include sex originated with the National Women's Party, which had been lobbying for an Equal Rights Amendment since 1923, and had sought to include sex in every civil rights bill considered by Congress over forty years. Despite the addition of sex as a protected category, the bill was passed in June 1964 by strong bipartisan majorities in both houses.

The Civil Rights Act of 1964 prohibits discrimination on the basis of race, color, sex, religion and national origin with respect to voter registration requirements (Title I), public accommodations engaged in interstate commerce (Title II), public facilities (Title III), racial segregation in schools (Title IV) and public funds (Title VI). Title VII prohibits unlawful discrimination by public and private employers, labor organizations and employment agencies. Constitutional challenges were raised quickly as to Congress' authority to legislate the act under the commerce clause but the Court upheld the Act.[135] The federal legislation creates a floor of rights under which the state legislation cannot fall.

The protected grounds have been expanded, with age discrimination added in 1967,[136] pregnancy as a subcategory of "sex" in 1978,[137] and disability in 1990.[138] "Sex" is defined under the act as including pregnancy, marital status and sexual harassment. The courts began almost immediately to dismantle the federal and state protective legislation passed restricting the work of women, invalidating lifting requirements as well as height and weight requirements for jobs traditionally held by men.[139] With respect to the protected class of sex, the Court

134 Kessler-Harris (2001) 242.

135 See *Heart of Atlanta Motel v. United States*, 379 U.S. 241 (1964).

136 Age Discrimination in Employment Act of 1967, 29 U.S.C. §§ 621–634.

137 Pregnancy Discrimination Act of 1978, 42 U.S.C. § 2000e(k). Sex includes pregnancy and marital status, *see* 29 C.F.R. § 1604.4 and 8, and sexual harassment, *see* 29 C.F.R. § 1604.11. Pregnancy was added by Congress in response to the Court's decision in *General Electric Co. v. Gilbert*, 429 U.S. 125 (1976). There the Court had rejected the EEOC guideline and the "heavy weight of authority in the federal courts of appeals", holding that Title VII did not prohibit discrimination on the basis of pregnancy-related conditions.

138 Americans with Disabilities Act of 1990, 42 U.S.C. §§ 12101–12117.

139 *See, e.g. Weeks v. Southern Bell Telephone & Telegraph Co.*, 408 F.2d 228 (5th Cir. 1969)(lifting requirement not a *bona fide* occupational qualification) and *Rosenfeld v. Southern Pacific Co.* 444 F.2d 1219 (9th Cir. 1971)(employer's policy to exclude women, generically, from certain positions on basis of strenuous physical demands of the positions both as to

has extended Title VII protections from simply the category of "sex" to a "sex-plus" hybrid theory of discrimination.[140] Certain other federal courts have also recognized "sex-plus" hybrid claims of discrimination including sex-plus race,[141] sex-plus age[142] as well as African-American women as a protected subclass under Title VII.[143] The EEOC has ruled that employment discrimination because an individual is transgender, due to gender identity, and/or because they have transitioned (or intend to transition) is discrimination based on sex, and thus violates Title VI.[144] However, Attorney General Jeffrey Sessions under the Trump administration has argued that Title VII discrimination protections do not include sexual orientation.[145]

---

hours of work and physical activity required with no showing that sexual characteristics of employee were crucial to successful performance of job, not a *bona fide* occupational qualification). These types of state statutes are now specifically addressed in 29 C.F.R. §1604.2(b)(1), Effect of sex-oriented State employment legislation:

"Many States have enacted laws or promulgated administrative regulations with respect to the employment of females. Among these laws are those which prohibit or limit the employment of females, *e.g.*, the employment of females in certain occupations, in jobs requiring the lifting or carrying of weights exceeding certain prescribed limits, during certain hours of the night, for more than a specified number of hours per day or per week, and for certain periods of time before and after childbirth. The Commission has found that such laws and regulations do not take into account the capacities, preferences, and abilities of individual females and, therefore, discriminate on the basis of sex. The Commission has concluded that such laws and regulations conflict with and are superseded by title VII of the Civil Rights Act of 1964. Accordingly, such laws will not be considered a defense to an otherwise established unlawful employment practice or as a basis for the application of the bona fide occupational qualification exception."

Much of this legislation was enacted by countries at the turn of the 20th century due to international pressures, such prohibitions as to working in certain sectors such as mining, night work and mandatory maternity leave.

140 *See Phillips v. Martin Marietta Corp.*, 400 U.S. 542 (1971)(upholding a discrimination claim challenging a policy not to accept women with pre-school aged children).

141 *See Jefferies v. Harris Cty. Community Ass'n*, 615 F.2d 1025 (5th Cir. 1980).

142 *See Hall v. Missouri Highway and Transportation Comm'n*, 995 F.Supp. 1001 (E.D.Mo. 1998).

143 *See Hicks v. Gates Rubber Co.*, 833 F.2d 1406 (10th Cir. 1987) and *Graham v. Bendix Corp.*, 585 F.Supp. 1036 (N.D.Ind. 1984).

144 *See Macy v. Dep't of Justice*, EEOC Appeal No. 0120120821 (Apr. 20, 2012).

145 *See* DOJ amicus brief in the case, *Melissa Zarda and William Allen Moore v. Altitude Express, Inc.*, 2nd Cir. dated 26 July 2017. Discrimination protections with respect to LGBTQIA issues are hotly contested at both the state and federal levels. On the federal level, the Supreme Court overruled its 1986 decision in *Bowers v. Hardwick*, 478 U.S. 186, which upheld a Georgia law criminalizing sodomy in 2003, concluding that laws making same-sex intimacy a crime "demea[n] the lives of homosexual persons", *see Lawrence v.*

Title VII makes it unlawful for an employer:

(1) to fail or refuse to hire or to discharge any individual, or otherwise to discriminate against any individual with respect to his compensation, terms, conditions, or privileges of employment, because of such individual's race, color, religion, sex, or national origin, or
(2) to limit, segregate, or classify his employees or applicants for employment in any way which would deprive or tend to deprive any individual of employment opportunities or otherwise adversely affect his status as an employee, because of such individual's race, color, religion, sex, or national origin.[146]

Employers of more than fifteen employees, employment agencies, as well as labor unions, are explicitly liable for discrimination under Title VII. A plaintiff must first file a charge with the EEOC or other authorized state agency before litigating a Title VII claim. To establish a *prima facie* case of Title VII discrimination, plaintiff must demonstrate using direct or indirect evidence that: (1) she was a member of a protected class; (2) she was subject to an adverse employment action; (3) she was qualified for the job; and (4) for the same or similar conduct, she was treated differently from similarly situated male employees. Once the plaintiff establishes a *prima facie* case, the burden shifts to the employer to produce a legitimate, non-discriminatory reason for the adverse employment action.

### Disparate Treatment versus Disparate Impact

Discrimination is not specifically defined in Title VII. The Court has set out two different methods of proving discrimination, disparate treatment (direct or

---

*Texas*, 539 U.S. 558 (2003). The federal Defense of Marriage Act, defining marriage for federal purposes as the union of one man and one woman and allowing states to refuse to recognize same-sex marriages granted under the laws of other states, was struck down by the Court in *United States v. Windsor*, 570 U.S.—, 133 S. Ct. 2675 (2013). The Court in *Obergefell et al. v. Hodges, Director, Ohio Department of Health, et al.*, 576 U.S.—, 135 S.Ct. 2071 (2015) held that the fundamental right to marry is guaranteed to same-sex couples by both the Due Process Clause and the Equal Protection Clause of the 14th Amendment. Approximately eighteen states have no legislative protections against discrimination on the basis of sexual orientation, *see* Jerome Hunt, A STATE-BY-STATE EXAMINATION OF NONDISCRIMINATION LAWS AND POLICIES—STATE NONDISCRIMINATION POLICIES FILL THE VOID BUT FEDERAL PROTECTIONS ARE STILL NEEDED (June 2012) available at the website of the Center for American Progress Action Fund, americanprogress.org.

146 Title VII, 42 U.S.C. § 2000e–2(a).

intentional discrimination)[147] and disparate impact (indirect discrimination).[148] Disparate treatment is the "most easily understood type of discrimination. The employer simply treats some people less favorably than others because of their race, color, religion, sex, or [other protected characteristic]."[149] Liability in a disparate treatment case "depends on whether the protected trait ... actually motivated the employer's decision."[150] In contrast, disparate impact claims involve employment practices that are facially neutral in their treatment of different groups, but that in fact fall more harshly on one group than another and cannot be justified by business necessity. Under a disparate impact theory of discrimination, "a facially neutral employment practice may be deemed [illegally discriminatory] without evidence of the employer's subjective intent to discriminate that is required in a 'disparate-treatment' case."[151]

The Court first invoked a disparate impact analysis in the 1971 case of *Griggs v. Duke Power Co.*,[152] seen by many as one of the most important discrimination cases since *Brown* as it empowered plaintiffs to reach the roots of discriminatory behavior.[153] The defendant employer in *Griggs* required either a high school education or an IQ test score for certain jobs. The Court found no significant relationship between these requirements and the jobs. These requirements excluded African-Americans at a higher rate than Anglo-Americans, and the jobs in question had historically only been filled by Anglo-Americans. The employer's requirements perpetuated the historical exclusion of African-Americans from such positions. The Court noted that Congress had "directed the thrust of the Act to the consequences of employment practices, not simply the motivation,"[154] and that the EEOC "had issued guidelines that accorded

147 Disparate treatment is based on section one of § 703(a) of Title VII, stating that it is unlawful for an employer (1) to fail or refuse to hire or to discharge any individual, or otherwise to discriminate against any individual with respect to his compensation, terms, conditions, or privileges of employment, because of such individual's race, color, religion, sex, or national origin, *see McDonnell Douglas Corp. v. Green*, 411 U.S. 792, 802–806 (1973).

148 Disparate impact is based on section two stating that it is unlawful for an employer (2) to limit, segregate, or classify his employees or applicants for employment in any way which would deprive or tend to deprive any individual of employment opportunities or otherwise adversely affect his status as an employee, because of such individual's race, color, religion, sex, or national origin, *see Griggs*, 401 U.S. 430–432.

149 *Raytheon Co. v. Hernandez*, 540 U.S. 44, 52 (2003) *citing Teamsters*, 431 U.S. 335.

150 Id.

151 Id. 53 *citing Wards Cove Packing v. Atonio*, 490 U.S. 642 (1989).

152 *Griggs v. Duke Power Co.*, 401 U.S. 424 (1971).

153 *See, e.g.*, Belton 174.

154 *See also Smith v. City of Jackson, Miss.*, 544 U.S. 228, 234 (2005) *citing Griggs*, 401 U.S. 425.

with our view." The Court held that § 703(a)(2) of Title VII did not require a showing of discriminatory intent. Under this same analysis, the Court later held in 1977 that a corrections facility could not have height or weight requirements for employment as a prison guard due to their disparate impact on women.[155]

In the landmark 1977 case of the *Teamsters*,[156] the Court addressed whether a broad systemic pattern of discrimination existed in the operation of the seniority system used by the labor union. Plaintiffs presented statistical evidence of wide disparities between the percentages of African-Americans in the work population at large in the community, and those employed by defendant in particular positions, with a total absence of African-Americans at certain levels. This was also supported by evidence of individual instances of discrimination. The combination of the statistical and individual evidence was sufficient to prove discrimination. The Court emphasized the inability of defendants to rebut an inference of discrimination based on the "inexorable zero," the total absence of a protected group from the jobs at issue.[157]

Disparate treatment cases can be brought by individual or multiple plaintiffs or as a class action. A claim of disparate treatment typically falls within one of four basic categories of proof: (1) direct evidence, (2) pretext cases, (3) evidence of mixed or dual motives, or (4) evidence of a pattern or practice of discrimination.[158] To establish a *prima facie* disparate impact claim based on evidence of a patter or practice, plaintiffs must show a specific, facially-neutral employment practice, a statistically significant disparity among members of different groups affected by the practice, and a causal nexus between the facially-neutral employment practice and the statistically significant disparity.[159] Disparate impact claims do not require proof of intent to discriminate. Statistical evidence consequently is often decisive to proving a disparate impact claim. Two rules of thumb have been used by the courts when assessing statistics, the EEOC four-fifths rule and the chi-square calculation. Under the EEOC Uniform Guidelines, a selection rate for any race, sex or ethnic group which is less than four-fifths of the rate for the group with the highest rate will generally be regarded by federal enforcement agencies as evidence of adverse

---

155 *Dothard v. Rawlinson*, 433 U.S. 321 (1977).

156 *See Int'l. Brotherhood of the Teamsters v. United States*, 431 U.S. 324, 335 n. 15 (1977).

157 *Teamsters*, 431 U.S. 342, note 23.

158 *See* Belton 68.

159 *See* Title VII, 42 U.S.C. §§ 2000e–2(a)-(k). *See also Johnson v. Uncle Ben's, Inc.*, 965 F.2d 1363, 1367 (5th Cir. 1992) and *Black Fire Fighters Ass'n v. City of Dallas*, 905 F.2d 63 (5th Cir. 1990).

impact.[160] In other words, if the dominant group of Anglo-American males is selected at a rate of 70%, any minority group with a selection rate for employment of less than 56% will be seen as discriminated against by the EEOC.[161] Chi-square statistical calculations examine the difference between what is expected and what is observed with respect to employment selection processes.[162]

### Shifting the Burden of Proof

Intentional discrimination, disparate treatment cases, can be based on an admission by a defendant, or a facially discriminatory employment policy, establishing the fact of intentional discrimination.[163] The burden of proof then shifts to the defendant employer to justify its reliance on the prohibited criterion. Such direct evidence of intentional discrimination is however rarely present. Most discrimination cases are proven through the disparate treatment doctrine, which relies on circumstantial evidence and a comparison of the claimant's treatment to that of another (possibly hypothetical) employee who has a favored identity status (such as white, or male, or in intersectional cases, both white and male). These cases are often analyzed under a burden-shifting framework as set out in the 1973 case, *McDonnell Douglas Corp.*[164] Under this framework, a plaintiff must first establish a *prima facie* case of discrimination based on indirect evidence.[165] Once it is shown that the employment standards are discriminatory in effect, the defendant must meet "the burden of showing that any given requirement (has) … a manifest relationship to the employment in question."[166] The employer satisfies its burden as long as it articulates a valid rationale for its decision. If the employer presents a legitimate, non-

---

160 29 C.F.R. § 1607.4D.

161 *See, e.g., Isabel v. City of Memphis*, 404 F.3d 404 (6th Cir. 2005)(African-American police sergeants with City of Memphis established *prima facie* case of discrimination through statistical evidence, including T- and Z-tests, that examination for promotion to lieutenant had adverse impact on them, even though passing rate under new cutoff score satisfied the EEOC's "four-fifths rule"); *Reid v. State of N.Y.*, 570 F.Supp. 1003 (S.D.N.Y. 1983) (Violation of "four-fifths rule" is evidence of adverse impact which would establish a *prima facie* case of Title VII discrimination under the Civil Rights Act of 1964, § 701 *et seq.*); and *United States v. City of Chicago*, 663 F.2d 1354 (7th Cir. 1981).

162 *See, e.g., NAACP v. City of Mansfield, Ohio*, 866 F.2d 162, 167–9 (6th Cir. 1989).

163 *See, e.g., United Automobile Workers v. Johnson Controls*, 499 U.S. 187 (1991)(defendant's policy prohibiting women, but not men, of child-bearing age from certain positions explicit facial discrimination).

164 *McDonnell Douglas*, 411 U.S. 792.

165 *See Texas Dept. of Community Affairs v. Burdine*, 450 U.S. 248, 252 (1981).

166 *See Dothard v. Rawlinson*, 433 U.S. 321 (1977).

discriminatory reason for the adverse action, plaintiff can only prevail by proving that "the legitimate reasons offered by the defendant were not its true reasons, but were a pretext for discrimination"[167] or by persuading the fact finder (judge or jury) that the evidence of discrimination was sufficiently strong to make it more likely than not that discrimination caused the adverse action.

By the late 1980's and early 1990's, civil rights activists and litigants were frustrated over the perceived inefficacy of Title VII, focusing on the inadequacy of the remedies and deterrence, as well as recent Court decisions narrowing the protections of the Act, arguing that the Court had seriously "misperceived the political will."[168] The Civil Rights Act of 1991 amending Title VII was in part Congress' response to the Court's decisions, particularly in *Wards Cove Packing* and *Price Waterhouse*.[169] The amendments negated these holdings by codifying the disparate impact theory of discrimination as originally articulated in *Griggs* and by amending the standard of proof required when an employer was found to have multiple motivations for an adverse action. Compensatory and punitive damages were also added to the panoply of remedies available to victims of intentional discrimination, with damage limits calibrated to employer size and after the 1991 amendment, Title VII cases are now eligible for jury trials.

### Title VII Remedies

Prior to the Civil Rights Act of 1991, Title VII plaintiffs were limited to equitable remedies.[170] Title VII now grants a right to compensatory and punitive damages awards in cases of "intentional discrimination," that is, cases that do not rely on the "disparate impact" theory of discrimination.[171] Punitive damages

---

167 *Burdine*, 450 U.S. 253 *citing McDonnell Douglas*, 411 U.S. 804.

168 EEOC, 40th *anniversary of the 1964 Civil Rights Act, Closing the Gaps—Making Title VII More Effective for All: Damages, Jury Trials, and the Civil Rights Act of 1991* (2004) *citing* Justice Blackmun's statement in *United Steelworkers v. Weber*, 443 U.S. 193, 216: "And if the Court has misperceived the political will, it has the assurance that because the question is statutory Congress may set a different course if it so chooses," available at the EEOC website, eeoc.gov.

169 42 U.S.C. § 1981 *et seq*. The Court had reformulated the standards and burdens of proof for a disparate impact claim, making it more difficult for plaintiffs to prevail, *see Wards Cove Packing Co., Inc. v. Atonio*, 490 U.S. 642 (1989) and held that even when a plaintiff proves that an adverse decision was made for discriminatory reasons, the employer can escape liability by proving it would have made the same decision even if it had not been motivated by discriminatory animus, *see Price Waterhouse v. Hopkins*, 490 U.S. 228 (1989).

170 *See U.S. Landgraf v. USI Film Prods.*, 511 U.S. 244, 252 (1994).

171 *See* 42 U.S.C. § 1981a(a)(1) and (b)(1).

are not available for disparate impact claims nor are compensatory damages other than in the form of back-pay and interest. Caps for compensatory and punitive damages are established on a sliding scale from $50 000 to $300 000 based on the size of the employer. Back pay, the amount awarded as compensation lost during the period between the triggering event and the judgment, and front pay commencing with the running of damages to the reinstatement of employment, are not subject to the damage caps.[172] A plaintiff must make an additional showing for punitive damages that the "respondent engaged in a discriminatory practice or discriminatory practices with malice or with reckless indifference to the federally protected rights of an aggrieved individual."[173]

### Title VII's Retaliation Provision

Title VII contains an anti-retaliation provision forbidding employers from taking retaliatory actions:

> It shall be an unlawful employment practice for an employer to discriminate against any of his employees or applicants for employment … because he has opposed any practice made an unlawful employment practice by this subchapter, or because he has made a charge, testified, assisted, or participated in any manner in an investigation, proceeding, or hearing under this subchapter.[174]

The issue was raised whether this protection was simply with respect to terms of employment or could be seen as broader. The Court in *Burlington Northern*[175] held that Title VII's substantive provision and its anti-retaliation provision were not coterminous, and that the application of the Title VII retaliation provision is not limited to an employer's actions that affect terms, conditions or status of employment, or those that occur at workplace. The scope of the retaliation provision's protections is broader than that of Title VII's substantive discrimination provision. The Court further held that the anti-retaliation provision does not protect an individual from all retaliation, but only from retaliation that produces an injury or harm. Plaintiff must show that a reasonable employee would have found the challenged action materially adverse, "which

172 *See Pollard v. E.I. du Pont de Nemours & Co.*, 532 U.S. 843 (2001).

173 *See Kolstad v. American Dental Ass'n*, 527 U.S. 526 (1999).

174 *See* Title VII, 42 U.S.C. § 2000e-3(a).

175 *See Burlington Northern and Santa Fe Railway Co. v. White*, 548 U.S. 53, 126 S.Ct. 2405 (2006).

in this context means it well might have 'dissuaded a reasonable worker from making or supporting a charge of discrimination'."[176]

### *Genetic Information Nondiscrimination Act*

The Genetic Information Nondiscrimination Act of 2008 ("GINA")[177] prohibits discrimination on the basis of genetic information by employers, employment agencies and labor organizations. Genetic information is defined as the results of the genetic tests of individuals or family members, or the manifestation of a disease or disorder in family members. A genetic test is an analysis of human DNA, RNA, chromosomes, proteins, or metabolites, that detects genotypes, mutations, or chromosomal changes.[178] It is an unlawful employment practice for an employer:

(1) to fail or refuse to hire, or to discharge, any employee, or otherwise to discriminate against any employee with respect to the compensation, terms, conditions, or privileges of employment of the employee, because of genetic information with respect to the employee; or
(2) to limit, segregate, or classify the employees of the employer in any way that would deprive or tend to deprive any employee of employment opportunities or otherwise adversely affect the status of the employee as an employee, because of genetic information with respect to the employee.

It is also an unlawful employment practice for an employer to request, require, or purchase genetic information with respect to an employee or a family member of the employee unless falling within one of the few listed exceptions.[179] Employers also have a duty of confidentiality with respect to an employee's genetic information. The remedies for discrimination on the basis of genetic

176 *Burlington Northern* 2414, *citing Washington v. Illinois Dept. of Revenue*, 420 F. 3d 658, 662 (7th Cir. 2005).

177 42 U.S.C. Chapter 21F, Prohibiting Employment Discrimination on the Basis of Genetic Information.

178 42 U.S.C. § 2000ff(7).

179 See *Jack Lowe and Dennis Reynolds v. Atlas Logistics Group Retail Services (Atlanta)*, LLC, 102 F.Supp.3d 1360 (N.D. Georgia 2015)(DNA test performed by employer on two employees to compare their genetic information with fecal matter in connection with defecation episodes, was violative of EEOC's regulation and warranted summary judgment in favor of employees; statute's plain language prohibiting employers from requesting genetic information from employees broadly defined genetic tests to include DNA tests of the type conducted).

information are the same as with Title VII and the EEOC is charged with enforcing GINA.[180]

### *The Federal EEOC*

The EEOC is the federal agency charged with enforcing the federal laws making it illegal to discriminate against a job applicant or employee on the basis of "race, color, religion, sex (including pregnancy, gender identity, and sexual orientation), national origin, age (40 or older), disability or genetic information" as well as with respect to unlawful retaliation for making discrimination claims.[181] The EEOC also issues administrative regulations and guidelines, working also with outreach, education and technical assistance.

The EEPC was created in 1965 to enforce Title VII, but not originally given the authority to litigate claims where the agency was unable to secure voluntary compliance. By 1971, it was apparent that the voluntary approach to Title VII was inadequate to the task of eliminating employment discrimination.[182] The Equal Employment Opportunity Act of 1972 strengthened Title VII's enforcement mechanisms, granting prosecuting authority to the EEOC. The EEOC also has the authority to prosecute claims under the Equal Pay Act as of 1979, the Pregnancy Discrimination Act as part of the Title VII and GINA. Individual must first file a Charge of Discrimination with the EEOC prior to commencing title VII litigation. Individuals, organizations, or agencies may file a charge on behalf of another person in order to protect the aggrieved person's identity. Mediation is typically the first step for each charge, and if not successful, the charge is given to an investigator. If the investigation finds no violation of the law, the individual is given a Notice of Right to Sue which allows litigation to be commenced. If a violation is found, the EEOC will attempt to reach a voluntary settlement with the employer. If no settlement can be reached, the case is referred to the EEOC legal staff or the Department of Justice, which then decide whether to file a lawsuit. If the decision is made not to file a lawsuit, the individual is then given a Notice of Right to Sue to pursue the claim. If a charge

---

180 States also have genetic privacy law, falling into one of three categories: requiring informed individual consent, restricting the use of genetic data by employers or insurance/care providers, and limiting redisclosure without individual consent, *see* Amalia R. Miller and Catherine Tucker, *Privacy Protection, Personalized Medicine and Genetic Testing, Study* (2015) and Atina Krajewska, *Genetic Nondiscrimination Legislation in the United States and Elsewhere—A Growing Body of Law and Its Impact on Employment*, Wiley Online Library (2017). Thirty-five states have legislation prohibiting employers from unlawful genetic discrimination.

181 For this listing of grounds, see the EEOC website, About EEOC, Overview at eeoc.gov.

182 *See* EEOC Annual Report 2005, available at its website, eeoc.gov.

appears to be groundless or have little chance of success, or if it is something that the EEOC does not the authority to investigate, the charge will simply be dismissed without an investigation or mediation.[183]

### *The Family and Medical Leave Act of 1993*

Federal legislation addressing issues balancing family and work came at a relatively later stage in 1993, and then only to an extremely limited extent when compared to European standards.[184] Protections are granted under the Family and Medical Leave Act of 1993 ("FMLA") with respect to taking unpaid leave from employment to care for family members for up to twelve weeks. The qualified medical and family reasons for taking the leave include the birth or adoption of a child, a serious heath condition of a family member or the employee, and qualifying exigencies arising from a family member's active military duty. Covered spouses under the act include spouses in same-sex marriages. The employee has the right to return to the same job or one very similar with respect to skills, terms, hours and wages.

The Hour and Wage Division ("WHD") within the DOL enforces the FMLA.[185] Both damages and equitable relief are available for violations of the FMLA.[186] An employer violating the act is liable for damages in the amount of any wages, salary, employment benefits, or other compensation denied or lost to such employee by reason of the violation, up to a sum equal to 12 weeks of wages or salary for the employee plus interest. Liquidated damages equal to the sum of the first amount including interest can also be awarded in cases of willful violations. Equitable relief can include employment, reinstatement, and promotion.[187] The statute also mandates an award of attorney's fees to prevailing plaintiffs.[188]

### *Presidential EO 11246*

President Roosevelt's Executive Order ("EO") 8802 was the first to prohibit discrimination on the basis of race, creed, color or national origin by federal

183 *See* Minawa Ebisui, Sean Cooney and Colin Fenwick (eds.), RESOLVING INDIVIDUAL LABOUR DISPUTES (ILO Geneva 2016) for reports as to the United States, the United Kingdom and Sweden concerning access to justice issues in pursuing employment claims.

184 Family and Medical Leave Act of 1993, 29 U.S.C. §§ 2601–2619, 2651–2654.

185 *See* the official website of the Hour and Wage Division and its annual Fact Sheets, dol.gov/esa/whd/.

186 FMLA, 29 U.S.C. § 2615.

187 *Id.* 29 U.S.C. § 2617.

188 *See McDonnell v. Miller Oil Co.*, 134 F.3d 638 (4th Cir. 1998).

contractors, as well as requiring that vocational and training programs were administered by such employers on an equal basis. President Johnson issued EO 11246 in 1965,[189] which included for the first time a prohibition against discrimination on the basis of sex for such federal contractors, as well as that such employers take affirmative action to "ensure that applicants are employed, and that employees are treated during employment, without regard to their race, color, religion, sex or national origin". President Bush amended EO 11246 to allow religiously- affiliated contractors to prefer individuals of a particular religion when making employment decisions. President Obama amended EO 11246 twice in 2014, first by EO 13665 to promote equal pay for women by improving transparency of wages and making gender pay disparities easier to identify, and by EO 13672 to prohibit federal contractors and subcontractors from discriminating on the basis of sexual orientation or gender identity.

EO 11246 sets out a holistic approach to employment discrimination that can be seen as comprising five prongs.[190] Federal contractor are not to discriminate against any employee or applicant for employment because of race, color, religion, sex, sexual orientation, gender identity, or national origin. The contractor is to take affirmative action to ensure that applicants are employed, and that employees are treated during employment, without regard to their race, color, religion, sex, sexual orientation, gender identity, or national origin. Such actions are to include, but not be limited to employment, upgrading, demotion, or transfer; recruitment or recruitment advertising; layoff or termination; rates of pay or other forms of compensation; and selection for training, including apprenticeship. These obligations are to be posed by the contractor in conspicuous places available to employees and job applicants. The contractor is also to state in all solicitations or advancements for employees that all qualified applicants will receive consideration for employment without regard to race, color, religion, sex, sexual orientation, gender identity, or national origin. Every contracting agency is also to include an equal opportunity clause in each of its nonexempt government contracts.

The Office of Federal Contract Compliance Programs ("OFCCP"), also within the DOL, is charged with enforcing EO 11246. The ultimate sanction for violations of EO 11246 is debarment—the loss of a company's federal contracts. A 2017 OFCCP "Glass Ceiling" audit of Texaco as to gender-based pay disparities led to a $3.1 million settlement for 186 Texaco female employees with back pay and salary increases, requiring Texaco to also annually analyze its pay scale and provide additional opportunities for its female employees.

189 3 C.F.R. § 339 (1965) and accompanying regulations, 41 C.F.R. § 60.

190 EO 11246 Subpart B § 202.

### *State Discrimination Legislation*

Discrimination protections can be also found on the state level in state constitutions, legislation and at common law. The vast majority of legal areas, criminal, tort, family and private law, fall to the jurisdiction of the states under the 10th Amendment, with each US state having its own constitution and legislation, as well as legislature, governor and judicial systems. In contrast to the EU, the US federal government has no mechanism by which to harmonize state law other than the budget. Federal legislation in areas in which Congress has concurrent jurisdiction with the state, in the question of discrimination protections based on the interstate commerce clause, acts as a floor with respect to state legal protections. States can choose to provide greater protection, but not less.

State constitutions clearly demonstrate the independence of the states to the federal system and to each other. Certain states have had only one constitution, while other states change or amend their constitutions more frequently. The span of different state constitutional discrimination protections can be seen in California (1879), New York (1938), Alaska (1956), Montana (1973), Louisiana (1975) and Rhode Island (1986). According to Section 8 of the California Constitution, a "person may not be disqualified from entering or pursuing a business, profession, vocation, or employment[191] because of sex, race, creed, color, or national or ethnic origin." Section 11 of the 1938 New York Constitution guarantees that "[n] o person shall, because of race, color, creed or religion, be subjected to any discrimination in his or her civil rights" by any other person or the state. Article 1(3) of the Alaskan Constitution (1956) guarantees that "[n]o person is to be denied the enjoyment of any civil or political right because of race, color, creed, sex,[192] or national origin." Article II of the 1973 Montana Constitution prescribes that neither the state or any other person "shall discriminate against any person in the exercise of his civil or political rights on account of race, color, sex, culture, social origin or condition, or political or religious ideas." Article 1 § 3 of the 1975 Louisiana Constitution states that "[n]o law shall discriminate against a person because of race or religious ideas, beliefs, or affiliations. No law shall arbitrarily, capriciously, or

191 The general tenet in employment law, which is mostly regulated at the state level, is at-will employment, in other words, an employer may discharge an employee at will, at any time, for any reason. Exceptions include, however, where the termination violates a contractual, statutory, or constitutional requirement (such as a prohibition as to unlawful discrimination), or where an employee is terminated for pursuing private statutory rights that are directly related to employment (as retaliation).

192 The ground of sex was added in 1972.

unreasonably discriminate against a person because of birth, age, sex, culture, physical condition, or political ideas or affiliations." Article 1 § 2 of the Rhode Island Constitution mandates that no one shall "solely by reason of race, gender or handicap be subject to discrimination by the state, its agents or any person or entity doing business with the state. Nothing in this section shall be construed to grant or secure any right relating to abortion or the funding thereof."

Many states also provide discrimination protections by statute. New York is an example of a state active early in passing discrimination legislation. Already in 1909, the Consolidated Laws banned discrimination because of race, creed or color in jury service, in the right to practice law, in admission to the public schools, and in places of public accommodation, resort or amusement.[193] From 1913 to 1935, the following were prohibited by law: different insurance rates and benefits as between white and colored persons;[194] discrimination due to race, color or creed in any public employment, or in any accommodation by innkeepers, common carriers or operators of amusement places, or by teachers or officers of public institutions of learning, or by cemetery associations;[195] inquiries concerning religion or religious affiliation of any person seeking employment or official position in public schools;[196] employment discrimination by utility companies on account of race, color or religion;[197] public contracts failing to include a clause against employment discrimination based on race or color,[198] and tax exemption to any education corporation or association which held itself out as non-sectarian but denied its facilities to any person because of race, color or religion.[199] The New York state constitution was amended in 1938 with the addition Section 11 as cited above.[200] Discrimination based on race, creed, color or religion under the public housing law was outlawed in 1939.[201] Labor organizations were forbidden by a 1940 law to deny membership or equal treatment because of race, color or creed; deprivation of public relief or work because of any such discrimination was also forbidden.[202] The state

193 N.Y. Civ. Rights Law §§ 13, 40, 41 (1909); N.Y. Judic. Law § 467 (1909) and N.Y. Educ. Law § 920 (1909).

194 N.Y. Pen. Law § 1191 (1913).

195 N.Y. Pen. Law § 514 (1918).

196 N.Y. Civ. Rights Law § 40–a (1932).

197 N.Y. Civ. Rights Law § 42 (1933).

198 N.Y. Labor Law § 220–e (1935).

199 N.Y. Tax Law § 4, subd. 6 (1935).

200 N.Y. Consr. Art. I, § 11 (1938).

201 N.Y. Pui. Housing Law § 223 (1939).

202 N.Y. Civ. Rights Law § 43; Pen. Law § 172a (1940).

forbade in 1941 any offense against Section 11 of the Bill of Rights, making it a misdemeanor;[203] and that same year, industries involved in defense contracts were prohibited from employment discrimination based on race, color, creed or national origin.[204] Discrimination in the sale or delivery of alcoholic beverages was outlawed in 1943.[205]

New York passed the Ives-Quinn Anti-Discrimination Law of 1945, one of the first state laws to prohibit discrimination by employers, labor organizations, employment agencies or other persons in employment on the basis of race, creed, color, or national origin. The law also established a permanent agency to enforce the legislation, the State Commission against Discrimination. The law was renamed in 1968 the Human Rights Law, and the State Commission against Discrimination was renamed the New York State Division of Human Rights. The law has been amended several times to add new grounds: sex (1968); disabilities (1984); families in the area of housing (1991); an express provision requiring reasonable accommodations in employment for persons with disabilities (1997); religious practices and religious observances (2002); sexual orientation (2003); and military status (2003). Obtaining employment, education, the use of places of public accommodation and the ownership, use and occupancy of housing accommodations and commercial space, "without discrimination because of age, race, creed, color, national origin, sexual orientation, military status, sex, marital status, or disability," is recognized and declared to be civil rights.[206]

Alaska presents another example of early legislation addressing discrimination, the Alaskan Anti-Discrimination Act of 1945, championed by an Alaskan Native-American, Tlingit[207] Elizabeth Wanamaker Peratrovich. The act was passed to combat the poverty and unemployment Native Alaskans suffered due to segregation in Alaska, banning discrimination in the provision of public accommodations to provide for "full and equal accommodations, facilities and privileges to all citizens in places of public accommodation within the jurisdiction of the Territory of Alaska; to provide penalties to violations:"

---

203 N.Y. Pen. Law §§ 700, 701 (1941).

204 N.Y. Civ. Rights Law § 44; N.Y. Pen. Law § 514 (1941).

205 N.Y. Alco. Bev. Cont. Law § 65 (1943). *See* Terry Lichtash, Ives-Quinn Act—The Law Against Discrimination, 19 (2) St. John's L. Rev. (April 1945), 170, fn. 2.

206 Article 15 of the Executive Law, Chapter 18 of the Consolidated Laws of New York § 291.

207 The T(h)lingit are Native American people in the Pacific Northwest coast. Lingit means "People of the Tides."

Be it enacted by the Legislature of the Territory of Alaska:

> Section 1: All citizens within the jurisdiction of the Territory of Alaska shall be entitled to the full and equal enjoyment of accommodations, advantages, facilities and privileges of public inns, restaurants, eating houses, hotels, soda fountains, soft drink parlors, taverns, roadhouses, barber shops, beauty parlors, bathrooms, resthouses, theaters, skating rinks, cafes, ice cream parlors, transportation companies, and all other conveyances and amusements, subject only to the conditions and limitations established by law and applicable alike to all citizens.[208]

This very detailed list of accommodations illustrates the depth of the apartheid systm in place against Native Alaskans at that time.

A modern example of state statutory discrimination protections can be seen with the Minnesota Human Rights Act ("MHRA").[209] The protected grounds under the MHRA are race, color, creed, religion, national origin, sex, marital status, disability, status with regard to public assistance, sexual orientation, and age, within employment, housing and real property, education, public accomodations (minus marital status, public assistance and age), and public services (minus age). The statute states that "[s]uch discrimination threatens the rights and privileges of the inhabitants of this state and menaces the institutions and foundations of democracy. It is also the public policy of this state to

208 When the bill was presented, territorial senator Allen Shattuck of Juneau had stated, "Who are these people, barely out of savagery, who want to associate with us whites, with 5,000 years of recorded civilization behind us?" Elizabeth Peratrovich spoke to the legislature during the vote: "I would not have expected that I, who am barely out of savagery, would have to remind gentlemen with five thousand years of recorded civilization behind them of our Bill or Rights." When a senator noted that a civil rights act would not end discrimination against Alaska Natives, she countered: "Do your laws against larceny and even murder prevent those crimes? No law will eliminate crimes but at least you as legislators can assert to the world that you recognize the evil of the present situation and speak your intent to help us overcome discrimination", *see* Daniel M. Cobb, Say We Are Nations: Documents of Politics and Protest in Indigenous America since 1887 (H. Eugene and Lillian Youngs Lehman Series)(Univ. North Carolina Press 2015).

209 MHRA, Minn.Stat. § 363A.01 *et seq.* Its predecessor was the Minnesota Fair Employment Practices Act passed in 1955 prohibiting discrimination in employment on the basis of race, color, creed, religion or national origin. The protected grounds of sex, marital status, disability, status with regard to public assistance were added in 1971 with the adoption of the MHRA. The MHRA was amended in 1993 to include sexual orientation as a protected ground, and in 2014, familial status was added. The MHRA is enforced by the Minnesota Department of Human Rights, *see* their website, state.mn.us/ebranch/dhr.

protect all persons from wholly unfounded charges of discrimination. Nothing in this chapter shall be interpreted as restricting the implementation of positive action programs to combat discrimination." The Minnesota Department of Human Rights enforces the Minnesota Human Rights Act and the Minnesota Department of Labor and Industry enforces the parental leave rights.

Another modern example is the California Fair Employment Practice Act, enacted originally in 1959, close in time to the first Minnesota Act, and recodified in 1980 as part of the Fair Employment & Housing Act.[210] Section 12920 declares that under the public policy of this state, it is "necessary to protect and safeguard the right and opportunity of all persons to seek, obtain, and hold employment without discrimination or abridgment on account of race, religious creed, color, national origin, ancestry, physical disability, mental disability, medical condition, genetic information, marital status, sex, gender, gender identity, gender expression, age, sexual orientation, or military and veteran status." One innovation under the California statute is a positive duty of California employers to "take all reasonable steps to prevent harassment or discrimination from occurring." Another was to lift all caps on compensatory and punitive damages in civil actions under the Act. The Department and Commission of Fair Employment and Housing enforce discrimination claims under the California Fair Employment and Housing Act, while the Employment Development Department enforces rights concerning paid parental leave.

### *Access to Justice Issues in the US*

The American federal and states legal systems are purposefully plaintiff-friendly, particularly when compared to many civil law jurisdictions. Plaintiffs are often permitted to file complaints based on belief and the parties are free to amend their pleadings up to a fairly late stage in the case management, however, not without showing cause after a pre-determined deadline as set out by the court's case schedule. The power of the courts to compel the parties with respect to discovery production is very strong, with the ultimate penalty for failure to comply with an order of a court is a party (or counsel) being held in contempt of court, subject to fines and/or imprisonment. Much of the federal and state discrimination legislation has record-keeping requirements as to hiring and employment practices facilitating evidentiary production.

Enforcement agencies are empowered to investigate claims on both the state and the federal levels. Congress also emphasized the importance of retaining a private right of action in the Title VII enforcement scheme: "The retention of the private right of action … is intended to make clear that an individual

210 The Fair Employment and Housing Act, California Gov't Code, § 12900 *et seq.*

aggrieved by a violation of Title VII should not be forced to abandon the claim merely because of a decision by the Commission or the Attorney General as the case may be, that there are insufficient grounds for the Government to file a complaint." Congress perceived it as paramount for the individual's rights to redress under the provisions of Title VII that all avenues be left open for quick and effective relief.[211]

The American rule with respect to the allocation of trial fees and costs is that each party is to bear its own legal expenses.[212] Congress has granted courts the power,[213] in their discretion, to award reasonable attorney's fees to plaintiffs in civil rights litigation, to ensure "effective access to the judicial process" for persons with civil rights grievances.[214] Accordingly, a prevailing plaintiff ordinarily is to recover attorney's fees unless special circumstances would render such an award unjust. The amount of fees awarded is to be assessed against certain factors.[215] A prevailing defendant may recover attorney's fees

---

211 *EEOC v. Associated Dry Goods Corp.*, 449 U.S. 590, note 21 (1981) *citing* 118 Cong.Rec. 7565 (1972).

212 For a discussion of this rule and its exceptions, *see* Gregory C. Sisk, *A Primer on Awards of Attorney's Fees against the Federal Government*, 25 Ariz.St.L.J. 733, 735 (Winter 1993). There currently are over 200 federally created statutory exceptions to the American Rule.

213 *See Alyeska Pipeline Serv. Co. v. Wilderness Soc.y*, 421 U.S. 240, 257–59 (1975). Under the common law private attorney general doctrine. the courts can award attorney's fees and costs in cases in which an individual plaintiff acted as a "private attorney general" in enforcing rights deemed to be important to the public. The Court in *Alyeska* held that federal courts could not use the private attorney general doctrine to award attorneys' fees to prevailing parties, stating that only the federal legislature had the authority to create exceptions to the American Rule by statute. The legislative response to this holding was the passage of the Civil Rights Attorney's Fees Awards Act of 1976, a statutory exception granting courts discretion in awarding attorneys' fees to prevailing parties in an action or proceeding to enforce a provision of a civil rights act including the EPA. For this history, *see* Jamie H. Kim, *Better Access to Justice, Better Access to Attorney's Fees, The Procedural Implications of Scarborough v. Principi*, 25 J. NAT'L A. ADMIN. L. JUDGES 583, 588 (2005).

214 42 U.S.C.A. § 1988. *See also Hensley v. Eckerhart*, 461 U.S. 424, 429 (1983) *citing* legislative history to the Civil Rights Attorney's Fees Awards Act of 1976, 42 U.S.C. § 1988, H.R.Rep. No. 94–1558 at 1 (1976).

215 The factors to be considered include: (1) the time and labor required; (2) the novelty and difficulty of the questions; (3) the skill requisite to perform the legal service properly; (4) the preclusion of employment by the attorney due to acceptance of the case; (5) the customary fee; (6) whether the fee is fixed or contingent; (7) time limitations imposed by the client or the circumstances; (8) the amount involved and the results obtained; (9) the experience, reputation, and ability of the attorneys; (10) the "undesirability" of the case; (11) the nature and length of the professional relationship with the client; and (12) awards in similar cases. *Hensley* at 429 note 3.

only where the lawsuit was vexatious, frivolous or brought to harass or embarrass the defendant.[216]

The statutes of limitations vary between the different discrimination acts, with Title VII having the shortest time span. A plaintiff is to file an employment discrimination charge under Title VII with the EEOC either 180 or 300 days after an "alleged unlawful employment practice occurred."[217] If a claim brought to the EEOC is dismissed, or within 180 days of filing the charge, no civil action has been filed, the EEOC must notify the plaintiff, who then has an additional period of ninety days after receiving such notice in the form of a "right to sue letter."[218] This 90 day period can be tolled in the event of an inadequate notice; in other words, the Court has found that the plaintiff must be able to understand the notice as given by the EEOC as to her rights.[219] The EPA and FMLA both require that claims be brought within two years after the cause of action arises, unless the violation is "willful," in which case a three-year limitation period applies.[220]

American courts can award damages as well as equitable remedies with respect to successful claims of discrimination. The highest EEOC discrimination award was for discrimination on the basis of disability in *EEOC v. Hill Country Farms*, with a $240 million jury verdict for 32 individuals with intellectual disabilities suffering twenty years of mistreatment by an employer. The breadth of remedies available for plaintiffs can be seen in the 2005 Consent Order issued in *EEOC v. Abercrombie & Fitch Stores, Inc.*[221] The defendant, a national clothing retailer with over 700 stores and 22,000 employees, was alleged to have engaged in a pattern or practice of race, color, national origin, and sex discrimination in the recruitment, hiring, assignment, promotion, and discharge of

216 *Hensley* at 429 note 2, *citing* H.R.Rep. No. 94–1558 at 7 (1976) and *Christianburg Garment Co. v. EEOC*, 434 U.S. 412, 421 (1978).

217 Title VII, 42 U.S.C. § 2000e-5(e)(1). *See National R.R. Passenger Corp. v. Morgan*, 536 U.S. 101 (2002).

218 Section 706(f)(1) of 42 U.S.C. § 2000e-5(e)(1).

219 *See Baldwin County Welcome Ctr. v. Brown*, 466 U.S. 147 (1984).

220 29 U.S.C. § 255(a) and 29 C.F.R. § 1620.33(b).

221 *EEOC v. Abercrombie & Fitch Stores, Inc.*, Case File No. 04-4731 (N.D.Cal. Apr. 14, 2005)(unpublished). For information about this, *see* the EEOC's Performance and Accountability Report for the Fiscal Year 2005, and the Press Release dated Nov. 18, 2004, EEOC Agrees to Landmark Resolution of Discrimination Case Against Abercrombie & Fitch, available at the EEOC website, eeoc.gov. In a later case, *Equal Employment Opportunity Commission v. Abercrombie & Fitch Stores*, 575 U.S.—(2015), the Court held that Abercrombie's failure to hire an applicant because she wore a head scarf for religious reasons was unlawful discrimination based on religion.

African-Americans, Asian Americans, Latinos, and women. Defendant centered its marketing efforts around an image it called "Classic All-American," targeting its recruitment efforts at white high schools and colleges and primarily white fraternities and sororities at the colleges. Defendant channeled minority hires to stock and night crew positions rather than sales associate positions, maintained a 60% to 40% ratio of male to female employees, and failed to hire and promote minorities and women into management positions. Defendant also terminated the employment of minorities and women when corporate representatives believed they were "overrepresented" at particular stores.

The consent decree, covering a period of six years, including the following conditions:

- Defendant's marketing materials taken as a whole are to reflect diversity as reflected by the major racial/ethnic minority populations of the United States;
- Defendant is to create an Office of Diversity headed by a Vice President who is to report directly to defendant's Chief Executive Officer or Chief Operating Officer;
- Defendant is to hire 25 full-time diversity recruiters;
- In consultation with an industrial organizational psychologist, defendant is to develop a recruitment and hiring protocol requiring that it affirmatively seek applications from qualified African-Americans, Asian Americans, and Latinos of both genders;
- Defendant is to advertise for in-store employment opportunities in periodicals or other media that target African-Americans, Asian Americans, and/or Latinos of both genders; attend minority job fairs and recruiting events; and use a diversity consultant to aid in identifying sources of qualified minority candidates;
- Percentage benchmarks are to be established for the selection of African-Americans, Asian Americans, Latinos, and women into sales associate, manager-in-training, assistant manager, and store manager/general manager positions; and
- The court is to appoint a monitor who is to prepare annual reports on defendant's compliance with the terms and objectives of the decree.

In addition, defendant is to establish a settlement fund of $40 million to provide monetary awards (15% back pay and 85% compensatory damages) to a settlement class consisting of African-Americans, Asian Americans, Latinos, and women who applied or were discouraged from applying for positions with defendant since 24 February 1999, and were not hired, or who were employed in one of defendant's stores for any length of time since that date. The consent order consequently includes as remedies damages and equitable remedies.

Access to justice issues, particularly punitive damages, are continually debated and adjusted within the US legal systems, on both federal and state levels. Given the view that individuals should be able to bring lawsuit to enforce the laws and rights, and the understanding that the law and particularly the courts are vehicles for social change, these issues will continue to be debated long into the future.

## Part 5: National Discrimination Legal Frameworks—The United Kingdom

England was the first country to become industrialized, almost a century prior to continental Europe, and the subsequent abuses and tensions in this new commodified labor market also manifested themselves at an earlier date than in the rest of Europe. At the same time, there was a prevalent belief in England at the end of the 17th century that the British were the freest people in Europe due to the 1688 Glorious Revolution. Many of those believing this belonged to the just over 5% of the population that had the right to vote, propertied male members of the Anglican church. Issues of race, slavery and colonialism, as well as of the rights of workers, women and children, began to be more publicly debated by the end of the 18th century, inspired in part by the American and French Revolutions, a growing wave of liberalism, Napoleon's march through Europe and the drafting of the Code Napoleon. Lord Mansfield declared in *Somerset* (1772) that slavery was not recognized within Britain and that the law favored freedom. Several British authors began calling for political and societal change, including Thomas Paine in the Rights of Man (1791) and Mary Wollstonecraft in A Vindication of the Rights of Woman (1792).

Initial legislative responses as to worker demands included the Treasonable and Seditious Practices Act[222] and the Seditious Meetings Act[223] of 1795, enacted to keep workers from meeting to strive for better work conditions. Several acts were passed in the next fifty years criminalizing certain worker actions in the effort to suppress protest and industrial action. By the mid-19th century, the socio-economic situation of certain workers was so egregious that employment protections began to be legislated, initially with respect to women and

222 1795 (36 Geo. 3) c. 7.

223 1795 (36 Geo. 3) c. 8.

children. A prohibition against women and children under the age of 10 working underground was passed in 1842, against women's night work in 1844, the limit of a ten-hour work day for predominantly female textile workers in 1847 and a ten-hour work day in general in 1867.[224]

Increased demands for an expansion of voting rights, mainly for men, led to several different voting reform acts. Women's voting rights were tied to the expanding rights for men, with women householders (widows and unmarried women of property) receiving the right to vote in municipal elections in 1869, and all men and women receiving the right to vote nationally in 1918. Advances as to education also paralleled this time line, with the right to primary education granted both girls and boys in 1869, and women granted the right to teach primary education in 1870. That same year, women householders could vote at school board elections and sit as members. The right to receive a university education was given to women in 1889, but full admission at Oxford was not given until 1923, Cambridge in 1947 and women's admittance to most of their colleges delayed until the 1970's.

The legal capacity of widows and unmarried women, *femme sole*, was never circumscribed by English law, however, the legal doctrine of coverture limited the legal rights of married women, *femme couverte*, giving husbands control of their wives' property. A series of Married Women's Property Acts, beginning in 1870 and culminating with the 1882 Act, abolished this doctrine, finally giving married women control of their own property.[225]

World Wars I and II brought about an influx in the number of immigrants to the United Kingdom ("UK") as well as a change in status for women. Women began to work, training to assist in the war efforts. To promote a continued peace after the war, the UK was one of the founding members of the Council of Europe, ratifying the European Convention in 1951, it becoming UK law with the enactment of the Human Rights Act 1998 in 2000.

The UK became a member of the EU in 1973. Under the Government of Margaret Thatcher, who viewed the EU as simply an economic cooperation, the expansion of the EU's social platform was contested. This resulted in a situation referred to as two-speed Europe, a period of approximately twenty years, where directives concerning social rights were initially taken with the exception of the United Kingdom of Great Britain and Northern Ireland, with

224 *See* Jane Lewis and Sonya O. Rose, *Let England Blush"—Protective Labor Legislation, 1820–1914* in Ulla Wikander, Alice Kessler-Harris, Jane Lewis, PROTECTING WOMEN—LABOR LEGISLATION IN EUROPE, THE UNITED STATES AND AUSTRALIA, 1880–1920 17, 235 (Univ. of Illinois Press 1995) 91.

225 This historical account is taken in part from Pamela Clayton, SOCIAL CITIZENSHIP AND POLITICAL RIGHTS OF WOMEN IN THE UNITED KINGDOM (Helsinki 1997).

a specific directive concern these two countries issued at a later date. As directives concerning social security and social protection required unanimous voting by the Council of Ministers, they could be blocked by a single member state, an option often invoked by the UK. Legislation concerning health and safety at work could instead be adopted by a qualified majority, and an example of this redirection can be seen with the 1992 Breastfeeding Directive concerning employment conditions, passed by a qualified majority vote.[226]

### *The Race Relations Acts 1965 and 1976*

The UK experienced growing racial tension exacerbated by the influx of immigrants after World War II, evidenced by the 1958 Notting Hill racist-motivated riots and the 1963 Bristol Omnibus Boycott taken to protest the company's policy of not hiring Blacks or Asians. The Race Relations Act 1965[227] was enacted as a response, prohibiting discrimination on the bases of color, race, or ethnic or national origins in places of public resort. The act also created the offense of "incitement to racial hatred."[228] A Race Relations Board was established in 1966 but with limited powers of mostly conciliation. Amendments were made in 1968[229] to strengthen the act, extending the discrimination protections to housing and employment.

The Race Relations Act 1976[230] replaced the 1965 act, and the Commission for Racial Equality replaced the Race Relations Board. The 1976 act was amended by the 2000 Race Relations (Amendment) Act to include a race equality duty. This public duty was in response to the Macpherson Report[231] on the unprovoked, racist murder of a black teenager, Stephen Lawrence by the police in 1993. At that time, public bodies were exempt from the prohibitions in 1976 act.

226 For this history, *see* Linda Hantrais, *The Social Dimension in EU and UK Policy Development: Shaping the Post-Brexit Legacy*, Working Paper CIS/2017/04, LSE Centre for International Studies 12 (2017).

227 The UK legislation is available at the UK Office of Public Sector Information website, opsi .gov.uk. For more information on the historical development of UK discrimination law, *see* Malcom Sargeant, DISCRIMINATION AND THE LAW (Routledge 2013).

228 Race Relations Act 1965, c 73. For a discussion as to the influence of US law on UK discrimination legislation, *see* Gráinne de Búrca, *The Trajectories of European and American Antidiscrimination Law*, 60(1) AM. J. COMP. L. 1–22 (2012).

229 Race Relations Act 1968, c. 71.

230 Race Relations Act 1976, c. 74.

231 Sir William MacPherson's inquiry into the matters arising from the death of Stephen Lawrence on 22 April 1993 to date, in order particularly to identify the lessons to be learned for the investigation and prosecution of racially motivated crimes: evidence submitted by the Home Office to the second part of the inquiry (1999).

The Race Relations Act 1976 has now been replaced by the Equality Act 2010 and the Commission for Racial Equality has been replaced by the Equality and Human Rights Commission.

### *The Equal Pay Act 1970*

Despite the significant entrance of women into the labor market in the 1940's due to World War II, it was not until the 1970's that legislation as to sex discrimination was enacted in the form of the Equal Pay Act 1970 and the Sex Discrimination Act 1975.[232] The Equal Pay Act 1970 was passed by a Labour Government, with the Conservative Government of 1970–1974 not bringing it into force so it was reenacted in 1975 as a Schedule to the Sex Discrimination Act once Labour was back in power. Under the Equal Pay Act 1970, women whose work is of equal value to that of men in the same employment are entitled to the benefit of a deemed equality clause in their contracts of employment. The equality clause was defined as a provision relating to the terms (whether or not concerned with pay) of a contract under which a woman was employed. If a woman's terms and conditions were less favourable than the equivalent term or condition of a man to whom they are compared, the woman was entitled to the benefit of that more favourable term, as if it had been included in her original contract of employment.[233] The clause was applied to redress imbalances existing in an employment contract between a man and a woman falling within one of five categories:

i. Like work;
ii. Work rated as equivalent by an analytical job evaluation study;
iii. Work that was proven to be equivalent outside such a job study;
iv. Work of equal value which is not similar and has not been rated as equivalent, but is of equal value in terms of demands such as effort, skill and decision-making:[234] and
v. Situations concerning wages while on maternity leave.[235]

---

232 *See, e.g.*, *Shields v. E. Coomes (Holdings) Ltd.* [1978] I.C.R. 1159, 1169 (Civ). The case also looks at the influence of the American Equal Pay Act of 1963 and federal case law on English law.

233 *See North and others v. Dumfries and Galloway Council* [2013] UKSC 45.

234 This category was added in 1983, *see* C. McCrudden, *Equal Pay for Work of Equal Value: the Equal Pay (Amendment) Regulations 1983*, 12(1) INDUSTRIAL L.J. 197–219 (1983).

235 The last category was added in 2005 to be in conformance with Community law and governed situations concerning pay raises and bonuses while on maternity leave and upon return from maternity leave.

In the absence of an explicit equality clause in an employment contract, such was deemed to exist in every UK employment contract. The employer's offered justification had a differentiated burden of proof depending upon which of these categories the unequal pay claims fell within. The Equal Pay Act 1970 was criticized for difficulties in application arising due to the inclusion of a real-life male comparator. The Court of Appeal in the case, *Alabaster v. Barclays Bank Plc*, decided after receiving a preliminary ruling from the ECJ[236] that less favorable treatment in comparison with a male comparator need not be proven in cases of pregnancy in accordance with Community law.[237] The Court in *Alabaster* found that the only appropriate way to proceed when faced with the paradox pregnancy presented was to "*disapply* those parts of section 1 of the Equal Pay Act 1970 which impose the requirements for a male comparator (Italics added)."[238] The Equal Pay Act was eventually replaced by the Equality Act 2010.

### *The Sex Discrimination Act 1975*

The Sex Discrimination Act 1975 prohibited direct and indirect discrimination against women and men. It comprised eight parts, with direct and indirect discrimination defined in Part I and with Part II addressing employment discrimination.[239] A person directly discriminated against a woman if he treated her less favorably than he treated or would treat a man. Indirect discrimination existed where an employer applied to her a provision, criterion or practice which he applied or would apply equally to a man, but:

236 *Alabaster v. Woolwich Plc* (Case 147/02) [2005] I.C.R. 695 (Civ).

237 *Alabaster v. Barclays Bank Plc (Formerly Woolwich Plc) and Another* [2005] I.C.R. 1246 (Civ). The plaintiff argued inequality in pay under the Employment Rights Act 1996, instead of the Equal Pay Act 1970 and the Sex Discrimination Act 1975, the first such argument of its kind. On appeal, plaintiff further honed her argument, maintaining that the Community principle of equality in addition to the principles of equivalence and effectiveness entailed that the right to full maternity pay fell within the ambit of Article 6 of the ECHR as adopted in the UK in the Human Rights Act.

238 *Id.* para. 37.

239 The eight parts were: Discrimination to which Act Applies (Part I), Discrimination by Employers (Part II), Discrimination in other fields: Education as well as Goods, facilities or services (Part III), Other unlawful acts including discriminatory practices, discriminatory advertisements and instructions and pressure to discriminate (Part IV), General Exceptions from Parts II to IV (Part V), Equal Opportunities Commission (Part VI), Enforcement (Part VII) and Supplemental Provisions (Part VIII).

- Which put or would put women at a particular disadvantage when compared with men;
- Which put her at that disadvantage; and
- Which he cannot show to be a proportionate means of achieving a legitimate aim.

This provision was to be read as applying equally to the treatment of men as of women except in cases of pregnancy or childbirth. Amendments in 2005 eased the burden of proof for the plaintiff as to disparate impact and heightened the employer's burden of proof regarding justifications in that the employer now had to show a proportionate means of achieving a legitimate aim. Protections against discrimination on the basis of gender reassignment and marital status were also incorporated, and pregnancy, maternal leave, harassments and sexual harassment were added by 2005 amendments. Protections against discrimination were extended to fixed-term contract workers as well as public office holders and persons seeking vocational training. Discrimination with respect to accepting a person as partner in a partnership was also prohibited. Labor unions, qualifying/certifying bodies, employment agencies, the police, prison officers and the Secretary of State were also prohibited from engaging in discriminatory conduct. An Equal Opportunities Commission was created under the 1975 Act to enforce it and the Equal Pay Act, which has now been replaced by the Equality and Human Rights Commission.

The Race Relations Act 1976, the Equal Pay Act 1970 and the Sex Discrimination Act 1975 were followed by a period of almost twenty years of legislative inactivity with respect to discrimination legislation. This perhaps is best explained by the Employment Minister's statement in 1992 regarding a prohibition concerning age discrimination: "More legislation is not the answer ... Sometimes we are accused of being reluctant Europeans because we do not believe that piling on regulation is the way forward. There are limits to the good that Governments can do though I sometimes think there are no limits to the harm."[240] The Employment Act 1989 removed many of the last vestiges of the protective employment legislation with respect to women in night work and mining.

240 Bryan D. Glass, *The British Resistance to Age Discrimination: Is it time to follow the U.S. Example?*, 16 COMP. LAB. L. J. 491, 509 note 95 (1995) *citing* UK: Employment Department—Ageism 'Shortsighted and Wasteful' Says Michael Forsyth, Hermes-UK Government Press Release, 14 May 1992. The statutory prohibitions against age discrimination was effected with the Human Rights Act 2006.

### *Disability Discrimination Act 1995*

The passage of the Disability Discrimination Act 1995 was to a great degree the result of the concerted efforts of civil society.[241] The British Council of Organisations of Disabled People, comprising over 100,000 full members, argued for a three-fold approach to improve the lives of individuals with disabilities: First was the need to develop a social model as a means to understanding disability. Second was the need for properly enforceable civil rights legislation to end discrimination against disabled people. Last was the demand for independent living, by which they meant being in control of their own services. The arguments and need for these three objectives were squarely addressed in a 1991 book authored by Colin Barnes, Disabled People in Britain and Discrimination: A Case for Anti-Discrimination Legislation. The Disability Discrimination Act was passed as the legislative response to the criticism raised by the group and the book.[242]

The Act prohibited discrimination against individuals with disabilities in employment, the provision of goods, facilities, services, education and transportation. Disability is defined as an impairment that has a substantial adverse effect on a person's ability to carry out normal day-to-day activities over the long-term. Discrimination was defined differently than in the other three existing discrimination acts, no longer a question of direct or indirect discrimination but of less favorable treatment and the failure to make a reasonable adjustment. A duty was imposed on employers and certain service providers to make reasonable adjustments. Case law has held that treating an able-bodied employee caring for a disabled child less favorably than another employee in a comparable situation was associative discrimination under the act.[243] The National Disability Council was established under the Act to oversee its enforcement, which was replaced in 1999 by the Disability Rights Commission. The 1995 act has now been replaced by the Equality Act 2010, and the Disability Rights Commission by the Equality and Human Rights Commission.

### *Human Rights Act 1998*

The Human Rights Act 1998 is the UK legislative enactment of the European Convention. Though it does not specifically address issues of discrimination

---

241 The EU directive prohibiting discrimination on the basis of disability was not passed until 2000, *see* Council Directive 2000/78/EC of 27 November 2000 establishing a general framework for equal treatment in employment and occupation,

242 *See* Mike Oliver, *Rewriting history: the case of the Disability Discrimination Act 1995*, 31(7) DISABILITY & SOCIETY 966–8 (2016).

243 *See EBR Attridge Law LLP & Anor v. Coleman* [2009] UKEAT 0071 09 3010 (30 October 2009).

in the workplace, several of the articles have been interpreted extensively to grant protection of certain fundamental rights, particularly Article 8 regarding the right to respect for private and family life, used to support protections for sexual orientation. Article 9 was invoked to give protections to religion. According to Article 14, the enjoyment of the rights granted in the Convention are to be secured without discrimination on the basis of "any ground such as sex, race, colour, language, religion, political or other opinion, national or social origin, association with a national minority, property, birth or other status." In the enactment the Convention, a provision was added in Section 3 that primary and secondary UK legislation "must be read and given effect in a way that is compatible with the Convention rights." Claims of sex discrimination and/or equal pay are often combined with claims under Union law as well as based on fundamental rights in accordance with the Convention as seen in *Alabaster*.

Grounds other than race, color, nationality, ethnic and national origin, sex and marital status began to receive regulative protection in accordance with the requirements of EU law, with the Employment Equality (Religion or Belief) Regulations 2003, the Employment Equality (Sexual Orientation) Regulations 2003, the Employment Equality (Age) Regulations 2006 and the Equality Act (Sexual Orientation) Regulations 2007.

### *The Equality Acts 2006 and 2010*

The Equality Act 2006 created a transition from individual pieces of discrimination legislation to their continued existence but within the act as an umbrella. The Act designated a list of "equality and human rights enactments" which the Secretary of State was empowered to add, remove or change.[244] The primary equality and human rights enactments were the Equal Pay Act 1970, the Sex Discrimination Act 1975, the Human Rights Act 1998, The Race Relations Act 1976, the Race Relations (Amendment) Act 2000 and the Disability Discrimination Act 1995. Sexual orientation, age and religious and political opinions were also listed as protected grounds for the first time by statute. The 2006 act created a "gender duty" for public authorities to promote gender equality and prevent sex discrimination in the exercise of public functions.[245] Service providers and public-sector employers were charged to design employment and services with the different needs of women and men in mind. A shift in enforcement emphasis occurred. Instead of individuals prosecuting complaints about sex discrimination, the duty placed the responsibility on public

244 *Id.* Sections 33(1) and 33(3).

245 *Id.* Section 82. This duty followed the introduction of a similar duty for race in 2000.

bodies to demonstrate that they treat men and women fairly and are taking active steps to promote gender equality, a form of gender mainstreaming. The three different governmental agencies charged with enforcement the individual acts were now combined into one agency, the Equality and Human Rights Commission.

The Equality Act 2010[246] continued the movement of the 2006 Act towards a more integrated human rights approach to discrimination protections, now no longer referring to other legislative enactments but instead consolidating the discrimination protections into one Act. The 2010 Act was the culmination of years of reform work on equality, finally bringing together all the regulations into one piece of legislation, and ironing out the existing inconsistencies. The act sets out discrimination protections with respect to services and public functions, premises, employment, occupational pension schemes, education and associations. Part 1 of the act sets out a public-sector duty regarding socio-economic inequalities, requiring the affected authorities, when making decisions of a strategic nature about how to exercise their functions, to have due regard to the desirability of exercising them in a way that is designed to reduce the inequalities of outcome which result from socio-economic disadvantage. This section however has not been brought into force. The protected characteristics under the 2010 Act are age, disability, gender reassignment, marriage and civil partnership, pregnancy and maternity, race, religion[247] or belief, sex and sexual orientation.[248] Protection is also extended explicitly to persons who are discriminated against based on association or perception.

Discrimination is defined as direct and indirect discrimination. Direct discrimination is defined as where person (A) discriminates against another (B) if, because of a protected characteristic, A treats B less favourably than A treats or would treat others. Indirect discrimination is defined as where person (A) discriminates against another (B) if A applies to B a provision, criterion or practice which is discriminatory in relation to a relevant protected characteristic of B's. The provision, criterion or practice is discriminatory in relation to a relevant protected characteristic of B's if

---

246 With limited exceptions, the Equality Act 2010 does not apply to Northern Ireland.

247 For more information on the protection of religion under the Equality Act 2010, *see* Lucy Vickers, Religious Freedom, Religious Discrimination and the Workplace (2nd ed. Hart 2016).

248 Same-sex marriage was recognized by law in England, Wales and Scotland in 2014, with Northern Ireland abstaining.

(a) A applies, or would apply, it to persons with whom B does not share the characteristic,
(b) it puts, or would put, persons with whom B shares the characteristic at a particular disadvantage when compared with persons with whom B does not share it,
(c) it puts, or would put, B at that disadvantage, and
(d) A cannot show it to be a proportionate means of achieving a legitimate aim.

Combined discrimination is included in the Act, but has never come into force. Combined discrimination is defined as where, "because of a combination of two relevant protected characteristics. A treats B less favorably than A treats or would treat a person who does not share either of those characteristics."

Harassment and retaliation/victimization within employment, education, services and public functions are also defined as discrimination. Employers are responsible for harassment by workers or third parties such as customers or students, if the employer knows that such harassment has occurred twice before and not taken reasonable steps to protect the worker from further harassment. The Act creates a duty of adjustment for disability.

A public sector equality duty exists under the Act, requiring public bodies, in the exercise of their functions, to have due regard to the need to eliminate discrimination, harassment and victimization, advance equality of opportunity and foster good relations between those who share or have different protected characteristics. This general equality duty replaced the race equality duty legislated in 2001, disability in 2006 and gender in 2007. The general duty is explained in that having due regard for advancing equality involves:

- Removing or minimizing disadvantages suffered by people due to their protected characteristics;
- Taking steps to meet the needs of people from protected groups where these are different from the needs of other people; and
- Encouraging people from protected groups to participate in public life or in other activities where their participation is disproportionately low.

The remedies are damages, including for injured feelings, and any remedy that can be granted in tort.

### *Parental Leave Discrimination Protections*

Early discrimination protections for UK women focused on facilitating women's family obligations and paid work, often in the form of part-time or fixed-term work. A second avenue of discrimination protections concerns the rights for parents as to combining work and family as found in several pieces of legislation. The Employment Rights Act of 1996 grants rights such as to parental leave and flexible working conditions, to paid time off for ante-natal care, time off for dependents when needed in order to make arrangements for the provision of care because of unexpected disruptions or termination of arrangements for care of a dependent, or to deal with an unexpected incident involving a child, during hours in which an educational establishment is responsible for the child. The employee has the obligation to inform the employer of the reason for the absence as soon as reasonably practicable as well as the expected length of absence. Suspension of work on maternity grounds is possible, but only if the employee continues to be employed by her employer, and is not provided work or does not perform the work she normally performs. If the employer has suitable alternative work available, the employee has the right to be offered this work before being suspended from work on maternity grounds. She has a right to remuneration by her employer while she is so suspended. Rights and obligations with respect to maternity and paternity leave are also included.

These protections were strengthened with the Work and Families Act 2006, which also extended the period of statutory maternity pay and adoption pay from 26 to 39 weeks and allowed the ordinary maternity leave and additional maternity leave to be taken for a combined 52 weeks without any length of service requirement. Entitlements to additional paternity leave under the 2006 act allow fathers to take 26 weeks leave as well as strengthening the rights of fathers to more closely mirror those of mothers. The Children and Families Act 2014 shows a further progression to the concept of parental, and not just maternal, care of children, with its Part 7 setting out the statutory rights to leave and pay, as well as the concept of shared parental leave. Part 8 addresses time off from work, and Part 9 the right to request flexible working.[249]

---

249 Other legal instruments setting out the regulations with respect to shared parental leave include the Shared Parental Leave Regulations 2014 (SI 2014/3050), Statutory Shared Parental Pay (General) Regulations 2014 (SI 2014/3051), Maternity and Adoption Leave (Curtailment of Statutory Rights to Leave) Regulations 2014 (SI 2014/3052), Statutory Maternity Pay and Statutory Adoption Pay (Curtailment) Regulations 2014 (SI 2014/3054), Shared Parental Leave Regulations 2014 (SI 2014/3050), Statutory Shared Parental Pay (General) Regulations 2014 (SI 2014/3051), Maternity and Adoption Leave (Curtailment of Statutory Rights to Leave) Regulations 2014 (SI 2014/3052) and Statutory Maternity Pay and Statutory Adoption Pay (Curtailment) Regulations 2014 (SI 2014/3054). The Equality Act 2010 also changed family law more generally by abolishing the rule of common law that a husband must maintain his wife, as well as the presumption that a husband is

### *The Equality and Human Rights Commission*

Each of the discrimination statutes had been enforced by an independent working commission, the Equal Opportunities Commission, the Commission for Racial Equality, and the Disability Rights Commission. The Equality Act 2006 dissolved these agencies and created the Equality and Human Rights Commission ("EHRC") in 2007.[250] The EHRC has the mandate to encourage and support the development of a society under which several objectives are set out, including where "people's ability to achieve their potential is not limited by prejudice or discrimination" and "each individual has an equal opportunity to participate in society."[251] The EHRC's primary functions are to monitor the effectiveness of the law and provide information, advice as well as educational opportunities. In addition, the new commission has the power to request information, conduct inquiries and investigations as to parties it suspects of unlawful conduct. The EHRC can serve an unlawful act notice upon parties it finds having committed an unlawful act, requiring them to draft an action plan to remedy the unlawful act or recommending an action to be taken by the party, but the Commission does not represent individuals pursuing claims of discrimination, but can financially support them.

### *Access to Justice Issues in the UK*

With respect to employee grievances against employers, recent legislative amendments[252] changed the thrust of employment dispute resolution processes from bringing claims at no cost to employment tribunals to first handling grievances at the workplace and if unsuccessful, the conciliation of claims. The United Kingdom Supreme Court held in 2017 that this employment tribunal fees system was unlawful as it impeded the constitutional right of access to justice and had to be quashed.[253]

---

presumed to be making a gift to his wife if he transfers property to her, or purchases property in her name. The Married Women's Property Act 1964 was also amended so that money and property derived from a housekeeping allowance was now to be treated gender neutrally, as provided by either of the spouses to be equally shared between them.

250 For more information on the Equality and Human Rights Commission, *see* its website, cehr.org.uk. The EHRC's budget was reviewed in 2012, with the proposal of reducing the spending amount of £ 62 million in 2008/2009 to £17 million in 2014/15.

251 Equality Act 2006 Part I Sections 3(a) and (d).

252 Mainly The Tribunals, Courts and Enforcement Act 2007 and The Employment Tribunals and Employment Appeal Tribunal Fees Order 2013.

253 *R (on the application of Unison) v. Lord Chancellor* [2017] UKSC 51 SC. Two fees were charged when bringing cases to the employment tribunals, issue and hearing fees. In a

The Advisory, Conciliation and Arbitration Services ("ACAS") has issued a statutory Code of Practice on Disciplinary and Grievance Procedures (2015)[254] to provide guidance for handling employment disciplinary and grievance situations. The Code emphasizes that fairness and transparency are to be present when dealing with such situations, including developing and using specific and clear written rules and procedures drafted by both employers and employees that are easily accessible. Grievances are to be raised and dealt with promptly, decided consistently, necessary investigations should be carried out, and employees should be allowed to be accompanied at grievance meetings. If unsuccessful informally, employees are to raise the matter formally and in writing, without unreasonable delay to a manager who is not the subject of the grievance, setting out the nature of the grievance. The code sets out a fairly detailed procedure to be followed with respect to the formal hearings in the form of procedural rules and the right for the employee to have a companion present.

Though not binding on employers or employees, the employment tribunals are legally required to take the ACAS Code of Practice into account where relevant when hearing a case. A tribunal can adjust any awards, made in relevant cases, upwards or downwards, by up to 25% for an unreasonable failure by either employer or employee to comply with any provisions of the code. A more detailed guide with respect to discipline and grievance issues has been issued by ACAS but the tribunals are not required to take it into consideration in relevant cases.

Before filing a claim with an employment tribunal, claimants are to first notify the Advisory, Conciliation and Arbitration Services ("ACAS") of the intention to claim so that ACAS can offer the opportunity to resolve the issue using a free process referred to as "Early Conciliation."[255] About thirty percent of those

---

discrimination claim case, the issue fee is £ 250 and the hearing fee is £ 950. The impact of the new fee structure was immediately dramatic, with the number of claims filed with the employment tribunals decreased by 78% within one year, *see* Ministry of Justice, *Review of the introduction of fees in the Employment Tribunals—Consultation on proposals for reform* 22 (January 2017).

254 The Code of Practice on Disciplinary and Grievance Procedures (2015) is issued under section 199 of TULR(C)A 1992, laid before both Houses of Parliament on 16 January 2015, and comes into effect by order of the Secretary of State on 11 March 2015, replacing the Code issued in 2009.

255 The Equality Advisory & Support Service ("EASS") provides public information and advice with respect to the Equality Act 2010, the Human Rights Act 1998 and discrimination claims on their website or by telephone.

using this process obtain a formal settlement, and of the unsuccessful cases, 17% decide not to pursue the claim further. Fifty percent went on to the formal proceedings, with thirty percent pursuing claims at the employment tribunal and 20% not pursuing the claims farther due to the high fees.[256]

If a case is then brought to an employment tribunal, a qualified (for seven years) barrister or solicitor acts as the Employment Judge. Two other law members representing the employer and employee sides can be on the panel if so directed by the judge.[257] Tribunals have an overriding statutory objective to deal with cases justly, which includes, so far as practical, ensuring that the parties are on an equal footing, saving expense, handling the case in ways that are proportionate to the complexity or importance of the issues, expeditiously and fairly.[258]

An employment tribunal decision can be appealed to the Employment Appeal Tribunal ("EAT") based on questions of law or absence of supporting evidence. Appeals are heard by an Employment Judge, unless the Judge directs otherwise and then two lay members sit on the panel. The issue can then be appealed to the Court of Appeal and ultimately to the Supreme Court (formerly to the House of Lords). Leave to appeal must be granted, and the object of the appeal is the original employment tribunal decision, not the EAT decision.

The allocation of trial costs and fees in cases before employment tribunals does not follow the English rule, but rather, each party bears its own costs and fees (the American rule). The tribunal can order a party at fault to pay the legal costs of the other party in certain cases where that party has acted vexatiously, abusively, disruptively or otherwise unreasonably during the proceedings, made a frivolous claim or failed to comply with an order. Legal aid is available for discrimination claims for individuals whose monthly income is less than £2,657 before taxes and having savings of less than £8,000. Union members can request legal assistance in their pursuit of employment grievances from their trade unions if such a provision exists in their Rule Book. The statutes of limitations for bringing discrimination claims vary from six months for a standard case under the Equality Act 2010 to nine months for a concealed case.

---

256 Matthew Downer, Carrie Harding, Shadi Ghezelayagh, Emily Fu and Marina Gkiza, *Evaluation of Acas Early Conciliation 2015* 65 (ACAS 04/15), available at the website of ACAS, acas.org.uk.

257 *See* the Employment Rights Act 1996, Employment Tribunals Act 1996 and Employment Rights Dispute Resolution Act 1998.

258 *See* The Employment Tribunals (Constitution and Rules of Procedure) Regulations 2004 No. 1861, Schedule 1, The Employment Tribunals Rules of Procedure, Regulation 16.

Remedies that can be awarded for unlawful discrimination include damages and equitable remedies. One example is a 2012 case in which damages were awarded for unlawful discrimination on the basis of race and sex. Defendants were ordered to pay nearly £4.5 million, including £1.1 million for loss of past and future earnings, £660,000 for loss of pension, £56,000 for psychiatric injury, £30,000 for injury to feelings and £4,000 for exemplary damages. The total compensation awarded was increased by 15% to take into account the employer's failure to comply with the statutory ACAS grievance procedure, and increased again to take into account plaintiff's tax liability as to the award.[259] Plaintiff was an obstetrician who was found by the Employment Tribunal to be subject to harassment and intimidation by senior employees before and during her maternity leave. She was placed on an unreasonably long period of suspension in 2006 before disciplinary proceedings against her began in 2007, and eventually she was dismissed in July 2008. The Employment Tribunal found the events leading to her dismissal comprised a concerted campaign to terminate her employment. As a result of that campaign, the Tribunal found that plaintiff suffered post-traumatic stress disorder, depression and anxiety leading to a personality change, and her husband had to quit his own job to care for her and their children.

The 2017 *Unison* decision by the UK Supreme Court held that the right of access to justice is both a constitutional common law right as well as a right under EU law and the European Convention of Human Rights based squarely on the rule of law: "Equally, although it is often desirable that claims arising out of alleged breaches of employment rights should be resolved by negotiation or mediation, those procedures can only work fairly and properly if they are backed up by the knowledge on both sides that a fair and just system of adjudication will be available if they fail. Otherwise, the party in the stronger bargaining position will always prevail."[260] Issues of access to justice, as demonstrated by *Unison* and the award above, are very much part of the discussion in the UK legal landscape with respect to questions of discrimination protections.

## Part 6: National Discrimination Legal Frameworks—Sweden

Sweden at the beginning of the 19th century still had very strong systems of both guild and state church control, as well as pervasive poverty, lacking

259 *Michalak v. Mid Yorkshire Hospital NHS Trust and others*, ET/1810815/2008.

260 *Unison* para. 72.

inward mobility.[261] Industrialism came to Sweden almost a century later than in England and the United States, but in the words of one author, it was "in record speed."[262] The legal and social structure of Sweden at this time did not allow women any legal capacity, whether married or single, with women objects of the guardianship of either fathers or husbands, and thus could not enter into contracts or even choose husbands.[263] Widows were granted legal capacity under the 1734 Code, but wives and unmarried women had none. Motions were made as early as the Parliament of 1809/1810 to grant women legal capacity at a certain age, the right to an equal inheritance and the right to participate in trade. These were made in part based upon economic necessity as there was a shortage of men[264] after recent wars, creating a surplus of "defenseless"[265] women having no male guardians or any economic means of

261 Statutes had been in effect for centuries regulating the master-servant relationship significantly to the advantage of the master, with the right to exert corporal punishment over wives, children and servants. This employment relationship was in the form of either a voluntary or involuntary (if a person was found indigent, to be without means) indentured servitude, first regulated by statute in 1664, with the last such statute adopted in 1833 and finally repealed in 1926. According to the *Lego Stadga för husbönder och tjenstehjon* (SFS 1833:33 p. 461) §§ 52 and 10, the master of the household could physically force servants to return to service and retain half of their wages as a sanction for fleeing. Servants could lose the entirety of wages earned for reasons such as negligence, laziness, slovenness, disobedience, ignorance or unsuitability, with references from the master reflecting such characteristics, making it impossible to leave.

262 Svante Nycander, MAKTEN ÖVER ARBETSMARKNADEN—ETT PERSPEKTIV PÅ SVERIGES 1900–TAL 89 (SNS 2002).

263 For a presentation of these Parliamentary measures and their treatment, as well as how the issue of women's rights became intertwined with the dismantling of the existing guild-system, *see* Gunnar Qvist, KVINNOFRÅGAN I SVERIGE 1809–1846 70–113 (Gothenburg 1960).

264 Sweden suffered a shortage of men during extensive parts of the 18th and 19th centuries. At its worst in the 1700's, there were five women to three men within the nobility class due mainly to military engagements. The shortage in the 19th century was due to wars, male emigration, and the longer life spans of women, *see* Karin Widerberg, KVINNOR KLASSER OCH LAGAR 1750–1980 23, 39 (LiberFörlag 1980).

265 Sweden had then four estates as reflected by the four chambers of Parliament, the nobility (0.5% of the population), clergy (0.9%), merchants (2%) and farmers. A legitimate child inherited citizenship, name and status from the father well into the 20th century. Individuals outside these estates had to prove economic self-sufficiency, with a presumption in the law that males working with farming had economic means, while servants (mostly women) were often found defenseless (*försvarslös*) under the law that in essence was a vagrancy statute. Being found defenseless could result in being sent to the work-

support. Allowing women to enter into trade was proposed as a better alternative than consigning them to prostitution or to the poor houses already filled to over-capacity.[266] Consequently, an equal right for women and men to inherit was legislated in 1845.

The first step towards liberalizing the economy was the Factory and Handwork Proclamation of 1846, taken in part in response to the motion for greater freedom of trade for women made in the 1809/1810 Parliament. Every person was given the right to freely create factory or handwork for his or her own needs. Swedish male citizens who had received the sanctity of communion could offer such goods for public sale, with women given a limited version of the rights granted men. Married women needed the consent of their husbands, their guardians, to enter into trade, a requirement that would be in place until 1920. Unmarried women had to be declared by the King to possess legal capacity.

Women and men began to leave the traditional employments in this transition from a medieval agrarian to a modern industrial society. The costs of industrialism in terms of human labor began to be debated in the second half of the 19th century. The focus of the Swedish Parliament at this time was on the employment conditions of children and all adults, not on women as a specific category. Motions were made as early as 1856 to limit the work day of all adults to twelve hours, and that of children under the age of 16 to eight hours. The opposition to such measures argued that such prohibitions would be an infringement as to the contractual freedom of the parties. A legislative proposal was adopted in 1881, containing a prohibition of the use of children and younger female adults in mines and quarries. An 1889 Act concerning Protection against Employment Dangers applicable to all workers regardless of sex was adopted, and a system of factory inspectors created.

The 1864 Freedom of Trade Proclamation finalized the dismantling of the guild system, expressly giving Swedish men and unmarried women the right to freely participate in trade or factory operations. Married women, however, continued to need the consent of their husbands. Unmarried women were successively granted legal capacity in 1858, 1863 and 1884. Women were granted the right to hold certain elementary school teaching positions in 1853, expanded in 1859 to a broader range of teaching positions and certain state jobs. Women received the right to privately-paid secondary education in 1870 and the right

---

house and women having no man through which to obtain economic sustenance were the most vulnerable in the system, *see* Qvist 44.

266 Qvist 80.

to university education in 1873. The first woman docent was appointed in 1883, and the first woman professor in 1884.[267] Both men and unmarried women who paid taxes were given the right to vote in municipal elections in 1862. The next year, unmarried women were given legal capacity automatically upon reaching the age of 25. Corporal discipline of wives by husbands was outlawed the year after. Women received the right in 1872 to choose their own husbands and married women were given the right in 1874 to dispose of their own income in limited ways, mainly for the purchase of food for the family.

The Parliamentary discussions during the 1890's show the beginning of a focus on women as a specific group needing legal protection in the form of employment restrictions. Sweden had sent a delegation to the Intergovernmental Conference held in Berlin in 1890 concerning worker protection and particularly the protection of children and women. Proposals were tendered for Swedish legislation forbidding the work of children and women in mines, quarries and other dangerous environments, as well as night work; and for women, work during the first four weeks after the birth of a child. Regarding a general limitation as to the work hours of adult females, the Swedish committee assessed that a limitation with respect to the work day of men was a more necessary measure. The most significant repercussion of the 1890 Berlin Conference in Sweden is the establishment of a framework for legislation limiting women's work due to their need for protection.

The first central labor union organization was established in 1898, the current central blue-collar employee organization, the Swedish Trade Union Confederation, *Landorganisationen* ("LO"), founded by the Social Democrats with the agenda of repealing laws impeding the organization of labor.[268] The issue of encouraging the organization of women in the labor was raised at the first Social Democrat Congress, with the response being: "As women's interests are shared with men and her participation in the labor movement would benefit the party and facilitate men's employment and battle against capital, the Congress encourages each proletarian woman to not be apathetic, but with all strength and energy participate in the fight and stand in solidarity with men."[269]

---

267 Sonja Kovalevsky, educated in Russia and Germany. The second female professor, Nanna Svartz, would not be appointed until 1937, the first female professor educated in Sweden, *see* JämO, VÅRA LÄROMÖDRAR OCH LÄROFÄDER, JÄMSTÄLLDHETSFÖRKÄMPAR I SVENSK HISTORIA FRÅN 1700–TALET TILL 1900–TALET 128 (2000).

268 *See* Presentation of LO, at the LO website, lo.se.

269 Yvonne Hirdman, DEN SOCIALISTISKA HEMMAFRUN OCH ANDRA KVINNOHISTORIER 39 (Stockholm 1992) *citing* SAP KONSTITUERANDE KONGRESSPROTOKOLL 1889.

The early 1900's was a period of excessive worker strife marked by decreasing wages and a general economic recession.[270] The first two national central organizations of employers were founded in 1902, the Swedish Metal Trades Employers' Association and the Swedish Employers' Confederation ("SAF"). The "December Compromise" was reached between employers and employees, represented by these three organizations, in 1906. In exchange for the right of the employer to freely lead and delegate work, hire and terminate workers, as well as hire workers regardless of union affiliation, the employers agreed to the freedom for workers to organize and take industrial action. The pattern of the social partners resolving labor conflicts without state involvement was laid by this agreement, with the social partners resistant to legislative control.

The beginning of the twentieth century, referred to by some as the "Masculine Renaissance,"[271] marks expansions in the rights of workers as a whole in Sweden as well as the beginning of restrictions of women's employment,[272] Three lines of restrictions were legislated, a mandatory unpaid leave for mothers in connection with childbirth, limitations in the types of work women could perform and as to night work with the ratification, mainly the result of the desire by Swedish politicians to be seen as offering the same amount of worker protection as other industrial, particularly European, countries. Sweden had sent delegations to the 1890 Berlin conference, the 1897 Zurich International Congress and the 1900 Paris Congress, congresses consisting predominantly of male representatives, all of which focused on the issue of protective legislation for children and women. The motivations for the legislation was to protect the weaker constitutions (and weaker understanding) of women and their duty to the home and future generations. These restrictions were incorporated in the Worker Protection Act of 1949.

The early 1920's had several positive legal developments for women. Married women received almost complete legal capacity in 1921 with the enactment of the new Marriage Code, heralded by certain Swedish organizations as the best in the world for furthering women's interests, with Sweden a model country

---

270 Birgitta Furuhagen (ed.), ÄVENTYRET SVERIGE—EN EKONOMISK OCH SOCIAL HISTORIA 73 (Stockholm 1993).

271 *See* Lynn Carlson, *The Beginning of the "Masculine Renaissance* in PROTECTING WOMEN 235.

272 A prevailing perception at this time was that the number of women in the workforce was increasing, while the statistics reveal the opposite, with women 30% of the industrial labor force in the 1870's, while in 1909, approximately 50 000 women worked in Swedish factories, constituting 19% of the industrial labor force, *see, e.g.* PROTECTING WOMEN.

for family legislation and a leader in women's issues.[273] Married women could now freely accept employment, or enter into trade without their husband's consent and suretyship as had still been under the 1864 Proclamation. Women were given the right to vote nationally in 1921 and the right of equal access to certain state employment in 1923 exempting, however, significant positions, such as the priesthood in the state church, certain military and diplomatic positions and positions responsible for the public order or safety. Access to the right of public employment for women coincided with a period in which men were leaving the low paying public sector jobs in favor of higher paying private sector jobs.[274] A system was also created in 1925 within state employment differentiating wages between men and women for the first time since women began to gain be employed in public jobs,[275] remaining in place until 1948.[276] A depression hit Sweden in the 1920's with unemployment reaching over 27%.[277] The same year as women were granted equal rights to public employment, a motion was introduced to restrict the right of married women to state employment. Motions were made in 1925, 1926 and 1927 for state action to encourage women to voluntarily terminate state employment upon marriage for the purpose of providing better income possibilities for men and unmarried women in order to help fight the rampant unemployment existing at the time.

### *The Swedish* Folkhemmet *and Labour Law Model*

The 1930's brought change, marking the birth of the Swedish welfare state, *folkhemmet*, and the finalization of the Swedish labor law model in response to the great labor unrest at the time, with over 700 strikes a year during the first half of the decade. The welfare state, comprising public services such as insurance, education and medical care, emerged parallel to the finishing of the labor law model, in many instances with the labor unions providing and authorizing social benefits, such as unemployment and sickness insurance. The central labor market organizations entered into the *Saltsjöbads* Agreement in

273 Karin Widerberg, KVINNANS RÄTTSLIGA OCH SOCIALA STÄLLNING I SVERIGE 1750–1976 115 (Lund 1978) *citing* Per Nyström, *Sveriges historia*, 5 I ORD OCH BILD 332, 334 (Sweden 1970).

274 *See* Renée Frangeur, YRKESKVINNA ELLER MAKTENS TJÄNARINNA? STRIDEN OM YRKESRÄTTEN FÖR GIFT KVINNOR I MELLANKRIGSTIDENS SVERIGE 59 (Lund 1998).

275 *See* Kjell Östberg, EFTER RÖSTRÄTTEN—KVINNORS UTRYMME EFTER DET DEMOKRATISKA GENOMBROTTET 107 (Stockholm 1997).

276 *See* Lotta Lerwall, KÖNSDISKRIMINERING—EN ANALYSIS AV NATIONELL OCH INTERNATIONELL RÄTT 64 (Iustus 2001).

277 Lars-Arne Norborg, SVERIGES HISTORIA UNDER 1800- OCH 1900- TALEN 70 (Almqvist & Wiksell 1995).

1938, reinforcing the Swedish model of cooperation between the social partners and the state's expressed policy of neutrality to labor issues. Revisions were made to the 1912 Worker Protection Act in 1931, prompted in part by the 1919 Washington Convention. Women were given the right to a six-week period of leave before the birth of a child without needing to demonstrate a health risk. Industrial female workers were now entitled to 56 days of economic compensation for maternal leave, while other female employees were entitled to 30 days, reflecting the difference between industrial workers having a mandatory maternal leave of six weeks and other female workers having no such requirement. A motherhood insurance system was created in 1931 to be administered by the labor union's health insurance funds, giving sickness benefits for 30–42 days as well as compensation to midwives. For those persons not eligible for monies from one of the labor unions' funds, a specific amount was made available. This was transformed in 1937 to a right to compensation for maternal leave based on general requirements.

Motions calling for restrictions as to the state employment of married women were again raised the 1930's during a period of economic depression caused in part by the Kreuger crash. Two government investigations, by the Population Committee and the Women's Employment Committee, respectively, addressed these questions and the employment of married women in general.[278] The Population Committee investigated issues concerning the low rates of marriage[279] and nativity,[280] and family structure in general. Alva Myrdal, chair of the committee, spoke of the significant *jämställdhet*[281] women had with men in the factories.[282] The committee proposed legislation prohibiting employers from terminating employment based upon marriage or

278 This debate was extensive, taken up by the different labor unions and other organizations. A men's union was even formed to fight against the injustices caused by married women having state employment positions, resulting in "double" employment within certain families, *see* Frangeur 196.

279 Sweden's marriage frequency reached an all-time low in 1930, *see* Qvist 18.

280 At the turn of the 20th century, approximately 260 children were born to each 1000 women of childbearing age, decreasing to 116 by 1930, *see* Widerberg (1980) 87.

281 *Jämställdhet*, equality between the sexes, was thus distinguished from all other forms of equality, *jämlikhet*, predominantly concerned at this time with equality between the economic/social classes, as well as within groups other than men and women. This conceptual distinction has carried over to other legislative areas such as discrimination based on race, disability and sexual orientation, all of which are referred to as issues of *jämlikhet*.

282 *See* SOU 1938:47 Betänkande angående gift kvinnas förvärvsarbete m.m. 64 ("Even within factory work, [women] have from the beginning taken a significant place *jämsides* with men").

pregnancy, as the Committee found that many women were choosing to not marry as marriage often resulted in employment termination. The proposal was enacted in 1939. Contraception was no longer outlawed after 1938. In a 1945 proposed amendment to strengthen the 1939 Act, it was estimated that as many as 10% of the abortions performed were motivated by a fear of losing employment.

The period following the 1930's into the 1970's is often characterized by the harmony reached between the social partners in the labor market. In contrast to their counterparts in England and the United States, women in Sweden were not brought into the workplace to any large extent during the world wars as Sweden maintained neutrality. The labor market participation of adult married women in Norway and Sweden during the 1940's and 1950's was at 5–10%, among the lowest in Western Europe at that time. Legislation mandating equal pay for equal work in the Swedish state public sector was passed in 1948 in line with the international instruments taking up the issues of equal remuneration for equal work. A general child allowance was established as a public benefit in 1947. Both parents were given legal custody of children in 1950 in contrast to the previous system of married fathers having sole legal custody. A national health insurance system was established in 1955. Women received the right to become priests in the Swedish state church in 1958.

Whether Sweden should ratify the 1951 ILO Convention No. 100 on equal remuneration, and the 1958 ILO Convention No. 111 on discrimination (employment and occupation) was raised in the 1950's. Both the social partners and parliament opposed ratification as they did not wish to depart from the generally accepted principle that the social partners, through free contract negotiations, had the right to enter into agreements as to wage conditions without interference or influence of the state. Different wage tariffs for men and women had existed in the collective agreements since the beginning of the 1900's. The central parties, SAF and LO, entered into an agreement that all such different wage tariffs would be phased out over a period of five years beginning in 1960 to prevent legislation in the area. Based on these efforts, the Government found that the conditions required to ratify the conventions existed in 1962, with parliamentary consent that same year despite continued opposition by LO and SAF. This voluntary phasing out of wage differences based on sex, however, did not effect a resolution of the wage differences between women and men. The designations of male and female employees in the collective agreements were often simply substituted with the new designations of "skilled" and "unskilled" workers respectively.[283]

283 *See* Lynn Roseberry, *Equal Rights and Discrimination Law in Scandinavia*, in STABILITY AND CHANGE IN NORDIC LABOUR LAW, 42 Scandinavian Studies in Law 223 (Stockholm

The increased demand for female labor participation in Sweden occurred during the post-war rebuilding phase in Europe.[284] Motions were made again in the 1960's to repeal the prohibitions concerning night work for women as preventing Swedish industry from maximizing its labor force, placing Sweden at a disadvantage among competing countries. Sweden was perceived of as losing the industrial advantage it had after the Second World War.[285] The dismantling of the statutory restrictions with respect to women's employment, once begun, took fifteen years to complete, beginning with the repeal of the prohibition of night work in 1962, the transformation of maternal leave from an obligation to a right in 1976 through the Parental Leave Act of 1976,[286] and the repeal of the prohibition of women working in mines and quarries with the passage of the Work Environment Act in 1977.

### *The 1970's: The Decade of Equality between Women and Men* (Jämställdhet)

Sweden was one of the wealthiest countries per capita in the world in the 1970's, capitalizing on an infrastructure left untouched due to its neutrality by two world wars. Europe was rebuilding, and Sweden provided many of the materials, tools and expertise. The 1809 Instrument of Government was replaced by a 1974 version, changing the balance of political power from separation of power to a separation of function. Parliament is the sole lawmaker as expressed in the portal paragraph of the 1974 Instrument of Government: "All public power in Sweden proceeds from the people." A comparatively weak judicial system was set out with limited powers.[287] The courts could declare a law in violation of the constitution in the case at hand, but were not given a power of judicial

---

2002). These new classifications have repercussions even today as jobs held by men are categorized to a greater degree and number than jobs held predominantly by women, resulting in very different wage development, *see* Självkritisk LO-bas lutar åt lagstiftad jämställdhet—För stark tro på reformer enligt Wanja Lundby-Wedin, SvD NÄRINGSLIV, 10 April 2005 1.

284 *See* Roseberry 221. *See also* Bengt Nilsson, KVINNOR I STATENS TJÄNST 290 (Uppsala 1996).

285 Motion 1960 (Second Chamber No. 26) 25.

286 Among the reasons Sweden maintains a top position with respect to sex equality in the international arena is its social welfare system, including the paid parental leave of eighteen months, the availability of inexpensive day care for children, free health care, as well as the number of women participating in politics. High degrees of both vertical and horizontal occupational and wage segregation, however, exist, *see* Statistics Sweden, WOMEN AND MEN IN SWEDEN (2016) at the SCB website, scb.se.

287 This is also clear from the fact that the third branch of political power after the legislative and executive branches, is the press.

review. With this focus on majoritarianism, only five articles on individual rights were originally included in 1974. After a change in government, the individual rights in Chapter 2 were expanded in 1976, including the addition of Article 15 stating that no law or other type of legal provision can entail that a citizen is treated less favorably on the basis of race, color or ethnic origin and Article 16 forbidding the state from discriminating against any person by law or regulation due to sex.[288] The role of these Chapter 2 rights, however, are greatly debated in certain circles, with some legal scholars in favor of a weak judicial system and Chapter 2 rights that are more a policy declaration not be to serve as a legal basis for a remedy.[289] The status of the European Convention in Swedish law was finally determined in two court judgments declaring that Sweden had a dualistic system and that the ECHR had not been transformed into Swedish law, and consequently individuals could not raise bring claims to Swedish courts under the Convention.[290]

The 1970's was the decade of change for women with the political campaign of *jamställdhet* and the transition to the economically independent women. Employment during the decade had increased by 390,000 jobs, of which 380,000 were held by women.[291] Half of all women working did so part-time, in contrast with 5% of men, and many women were working in the rapidly expanding public sector. The level of occupational segregation was high as were wage differences between women and men, at least in part a relic of the different tariffs that had explicitly existed in certain collective agreements until the mid-1970's. Women still had almost total responsibility in the private sphere for home and the care of children. The word *jämställdhet* began to be used in earnest, coined to denote a demarcation from equality in society as whole, *jämlikhet*. *Jämställdhet* focused exclusively on equality between the sexes, marking a shift from women's issues to societal issues between women and men. Theoretically this was to free both sexes from the roles that society historically had placed on them, giving women and men equal rights as well as equal responsibilities. To this end, one of the first acts with respect to *jämställdhet*

288 Exceptions to this were included in the article, however, in that the discrimination is to be deemed legal if the legal instrument constitutes a step in the endeavor to achieve equality between men and women or unless it relates to compulsory military service or other similar official duties.

289 A 2017 legislative bill has been introduced to allow for damages to be awarded in cases of violations of the ECHR and the Swedish constitution by the state, with the first case doing so for a violation of the ECHR decided in 2005, *see* Lundgren judgment, NJA 2005 p. 462.

290 *See* NJA 1973 p. 423 and RÅ 1974 p. 121.

291 *See* SOU 1978:38 39 and Prop. 1978/79:175 med förslag till lag om jämställdhet mellan kvinnor och män i arbetslivet, m.m. 13–15.

was the transition from family-based to individual income taxation in 1972, a process completed by 1991.[292]

The second step in this movement to economically independent women were amendments to the Marriage Code and the virtual repeal as to spousal maintenance after marital dissolution, reflecting in part an ideological shift from the single breadwinner provider to a two-income household. The objective set out in the Marriage Code is that spouses are to be economically self-sufficient. Each spouse has legal control of his or her property and is responsible for his or her own debts. Spouses have a legal duty to provide each other with the information necessary for assessment of the family's financial condition. In the event a spouse is not able economically to support his or her own personal needs, the other spouse has a legal duty to provide that which is reasonably needed. Spousal property is marital property to be shared equally upon dissolution based on marital divorce or death, unless the property is designated as individual property.[293] Individual property is either defined either by law or declared as such by the spouse, employer or any donor of gifts and as a rule, incomes, insurances and pensions are individual property. The other spouse can make no claim on individual property, or on any future income. Individual property is not included in the marital estate, and the only deviation allowed from a 50/50 division of the marital property is one in favor of the wealthier spouse, as he or she should not be forced to contribute more than found just according to the Marriage Code. A right to spousal maintenance still technically exists,[294] but the dividing line between awarding spousal maintenance or not is basically destitution, the driving force being that the state should not then have to support a former spouse. Spouses have no

---

292 Wealth tax, however, is still assessed on a family basis. For a criticism of the theoretical neutrality of this taxation system and its contribution to *jämställdhet*, *see* Åsa Gunnarsson, *Myten om vad den könsneutrala skatterätten kan göra för jämställdheten*, 2000 SKATTENYTT 487.

293 Swedish law does not recognize joint tenancy property ownership, only tenants in common. The latter is a fairly rare outside of real property ownership.

294 *Id. citing* Anders Agell, UNDERHÅLL TILL BARN OCH MAKE (4th ed. 1988) 102 and Prop. 1978/79:12 *om underhåll till barn och frånskilda, m.m.* The obligation as to spousal maintenance arguably never took root in the Swedish case law even when it did exist. Already at the beginning of the 1970's when the wage gap between women and men was ignificant and many women did not yet work or only worked part-time, spousal maintenance was awarded on a national average in one out of ten cases, and half of these for a period of four years or less, *see* Anders Agell, ÄKTENSKAP SAMBOENDE PARTNERSKAP 54 (3rd ed. Iustus 2004).

right to claims of maintaining the same standard of living upon dissolution.[295] These limited rights as to the marital estate are only granted to married spouses or registered partners, while almost one-third of the couples in Sweden cohabit and consequently fall outside these rights.[296]

Another significant legal event in the 1970's was the passage of a package of labor law legislation, in part codifying certain practices in the collective agreements, but also for the objective of creating greater democracy at the workplace. One of the first acts was on employment protection (1974), with the last the Equal Treatment between Women and Men at Work (1979).[297] The issue of whether legislation should be used as a means to promote equality between women and men had been the object of general debate during the entirety of the 1970's. Proposals for legislation as well as calls for government investigations as to sex discrimination were raised in several motions to the Swedish Parliament by the liberal political party, *Folkpartiet*.[298] The original motions included prohibitions against unlawful discrimination on other grounds, such as race, based on the American federal Civil Rights Act of 1964. An Equality Delegation was appointed, presenting its conclusions in 1975 that legislation could easily freeze the current injustices in the system and impede more active equality measures.[299] The delegation found overwhelming reasons against adopting legislation similar to that in the United States. The statutory regulation of discrimination in the private sector was also long fought by both employer and employee organizations. The social partners argued that discrimination did not and should not differ in any aspect from other em-

---

295 It was noted at the time of the passage of these amendments that the economic situation of women after divorce was worse, *see, e.g.*, Prop. 1978/79:12 70. The economic repercussions of this system combined with employment decisions are most palpable with pensions. Many, if not most, Swedish women take most of the extended parental leave, working part-time usually after. In 2016, women had 67% of men's pensions, *see* Statistics Sweden scb.se.

296 As to property regimes based on marriage or cohabitation in Sweden and the United States, *see* Göran Lind, COMMON LAW MARRIAGE—A LEGAL INSTITUTE FOR COHABITATION (Oxford 2008).

297 The package include legislation governing working hours in general and specifically household work in 1970, in 1974 acts on employment protection, trade union representatives, a right to unpaid employment leave for educational purposes and the Labour Disputes (Judicial Procedure) Act. The Employment (Co-determination in the Workplace) Act and Parental Leave Act were passed in 1976.

298 Legislative Bill 1978/79:175 med förslag till lag om jämställdhet mellan kvinnor och män i arbetslivet 9.

299 Ds Ju 1975:7 *PM till frågan om lagstiftning mot könsdiskriminering.*

ployment issues as already falling within their self-regulation under the labor law model.[300]

Sweden participated in the first United Nations World Conference of Women in 1975, resulting in another international push towards legislation prohibiting discrimination on the basis of sex. After a change of Government, another Equality Committee was appointed with a mandate based on the conviction that a law prohibiting sex discrimination was significant as one of several societal mechanisms for bringing about societal change.[301] In response, the social partners entered into an Equality Agreement in 1977 covering large segments of the private sector, all areas except transportation in an effort to prevent later regulation by the proposed statute or Equal Opportunity between Women and Men Ombudsman ("*JämO*"). The social partners then argued that these agreements should be given time to assess their effectiveness prior to any adoption of legislation. In the alternative, the social partners argued that legislation would impede work with equality and increase bureaucracy.[302]

### *The 1979 Equality between Women and Men Act*

The second Equality Committee issued its report in 1978 and the Government thereafter presented a first legislative bill with respect to prohibiting unlawful sex discrimination in employment. Only a "half-law" was initially passed by the parliament with a vote of 155 to 150, namely simply the paragraphs in the legislative bill containing the general prohibition against discrimination.[303] The proposed parts covering the Equal Opportunity Ombudsman, *JämO*, as well as active measures, were not adopted. Strong resistance existed as to placing collective agreements within the jurisdiction of *JämO*. A second legislative bill, largely identical to the first, was adopted in its entirety in 1979, passing by only one vote.[304] After decades of discussion and debate, the first Swedish

300 Legislative Bill 1978/79:175 *med förslag till lag om jämställdhet mellan kvinnor och män i arbetslivet, m.m.* 25. All the social partners were negative to the proposal with the exception of SACO/SR, *id.* 196.

301 *See* SOU 1975:58 *Målet är jämställdhet.*

302 *See* Legislative Bill 1978/79:56 *med förslag till lag om jämställdhet mellan kvinnor och män i arbetslivet*, 9 and 196.

303 *See* SOU 1978:38 *Jämställdhet i arbetslivet med förslag till lag om jämställdhet mellan kvinnor och män i arbetslivet*; Legislative Bill 1978/79:175 *med förslag till lag om jämställdhet mellan kvinnor och män i arbetslivet, m.m.*; and *Lag* (1979:503) *om jämställdhet mellan kvinnor och män i arbetslivet.*

304 Legislative Bill 1979/80:56 *med förslag till lag om jämställdhet mellan kvinnor och män i arbetslivet, m.m.*, and Nycander 375.

act prohibiting unequal treatment of women and men in work finally came to pass, effective 1 July 1980.[305]

The 1979 Equal Treatment Act had three components: discrimination prohibitions, active measures to be taken by employers, and enforcement mechanisms and procedures, including the establishment of *JämO*. The social partners could derogate from the statutory active measures through collective agreements. Damages could be awarded for violations of the Act with a "group rebate" created in the event an employer discriminated against more than the one person, the damages then were to be assessed for one person to be shared equally by the group. That the 1979 Equal Treatment Act was not a happy compromise can be seen not only from the fact that it only passed by one vote, but also from its many amendments. The act was amended rather significantly already by 1980 in part due to Sweden signing CEDAW.

Pressured by its international obligations and criticisms for the failures to implement them, the first act prohibiting discrimination on the basis of ethnic origins was passed in 1986.[306] Containing only seven paragraphs, it prohibited ethnic discrimination based on race, color, nationality, ethnic origins or religion. The office of an Ombudsman against Ethnic Discrimination was created to work towards preventing ethnic discrimination in employment and other societal areas. Although technically legislation, no sanctions were included in the act and consequently, plaintiffs had no right to any remedies under the act and no cases were brought. The late date of this first act prohibiting race discrimination[307] is also telling given the fact that several ethnic groups have historically been treated differently to their disadvantage under Swedish law, such as the Sami, Romani and Jews. Theories of eugenics had great influence in Sweden in the first half of the 20th century, resulting in different statutory treatment, and the objectification of certain groups. This influence can be seen for example, in political discussions regarding the Sami, which earlier had focused on low (Sami) and high (Swedish) culture. The nuances changed in the early 20th century to a focus on superior (Swedish) and inferior (Sami) races.[308] Education for the Sami was not to be as extensive as for ethnic-Swedes ac-

305 *Lag* (1979:1118) *om jämställdhet mellan kvinnor och män i arbetslivet.*

306 *Lag* (1986:442) *mot etnisk diskriminering.*

307 Sweden has had a long history with the term "race" that can be traced back to Carl Linnaeus, the father of modern taxonomy. Linnaeus used the term "ras" in his work, Systema naturae, published in 1735 to categorize human beings into five groups: Africanus, Americanus, Asiaticus, Europeanus and Monstrosus.

308 The State Institution for Racial Hygiene (*Statens institut för rashygien*) was established in Uppsala in 1922, becoming the first state-funded race institution in the world.

cording to the legislative preparatory works to the 1913 act on a specific nomad school, as the "Sami were to remain Sami" (*lapp ska vara lapp*).[309] A child attending a nomad school was not eligible for university studies. A 1928 act prescribed that those Sami not participating in traditional reindeer-herding could not claim any other Sami rights, such as rights to fishing or hunting.[310] Discrimination against the Romani, anti-zyganism, can be traced back to the 16th century.[311] In modern times, it was forbidden for the Romani to migrant to Sweden from 1914 until after World War II, 1954 when the ban was lifted. The period of this ban coincided with Hitler's persecution of the Romani. A subtle change occurred after World War II, and the explicitly discriminatory laws began to be repealed. One example is that the 1951 Religious Freedom Act gave Swedish citizens the right to freely leave the state Lutheran Church, and it then became voluntary for Jews to belong to a synagogue. It would not be until 1999 that a claim of discrimination on the basis of ethnicity could be raised to a court, and not until 2002 that the Labour Court would find unlawful ethnic discrimination.[312] The Swedish legislature removed the word "race" from the 2008 Discrimination Act.

Involuntary sterilizations began with the eugenics program of the Swedish Race Institute in the 1934, targeting certain groups, which law was in effect until 1976. Initially the groups targeted were persons with mental disabilities or those considered asocial, but expanded later to include other social problems. Young women having children outside of marriage consented to "voluntary" sterilization when the threat was made as pulling social benefits, particularly to Romani women. The three indicators used by physicians to assess the need for sterilization were eugenic, social and medicinal, originally with no

---

309 *See* SOU 1960:41, SAMERNAS SKOLGÅNG 38 (1957). For the discussion on eugenics and the Sami, *see* Erik-Oscar Oscarsson, RASTÄNKANDE OCH SÄRSKILJANDE AV SAMER 942 (2016).

310 When the Instrument of Government was amended in 1976 to give greater discrimination protections and the Sami were recognized by Sweden as an indigenous people under international law in 1977, a group of Sami brought a lawsuit legal rights as to reindeer herding. The Swedish Supreme Court held that there may have been a different treatment of the Sami in the case, but as there was no other group that could be used as a comparator with respect to these question, no unlawful discrimination could be found, *see Skattefjäll case*, NJA 1981 p. 1. The Supreme Court addressed a similar issue again in 2011 as to reindeer herding and Sami rights, but this time found for the Sami, *Nordmaling case*, NJA 2011 p. 109.

311 Ombudsmannen mot Etnisk Diskriminering, DISKRIMINERING AV ROMER I SVERIGE 7 (DO 2004).

312 *See* AD 2002 no. 128.

administrative procedures in place as to the decisions taken. The law was amended in the 1950's to include procedural rights, and the eugenics motivation for sterilizations became less utilized. Estimates are that 63,000 thousand individuals were sterilized in the period from 1934 to 1976. Approximately 1,600 individuals have received damages of SEK 175,000 from the state in the limited window of time allowed for such claims between 2000–2003.[313]

This belief in eugenics and social engineering also led to the removal of children from homes. The 1924 Involuntary Child Care act was amended to allow children to be taken into state care where there was a risk that the parents had mental disabilities, immoral lives or were not industrious.[314] At least one-quarter of a million children were placed in foster homes or institutions at some point between 1920–1995, at times when Sweden's total population varied between six and nine million respectively. Reparations by the State for the abuse and neglect suffered by those children removed from their families during the period from 1920 to 1980 was offered 2012–2014 in the amount of SEK 250,000 per child.[315]

Sweden was the first nation in 1972 to pass an act concerning gender reassignment, which governed both legal and medical gender reassignment, and required sterilization for gender reassignment.[316] The Administrative Court of Appeals held in 2012 that this requirement of involuntary sterilization was a violation and discrimination under both the Instrument of Government and the ECHR.[317] The legal requirement of sterilization was removed by law in 2013. It is estimated that approximately 800 individuals were forced to undergo sterilization for gender reassignment in the period from 1972–2013. Sweden has now recognized this requirement as a violation of human rights and is in the process of setting up a compensation program, in April 2017 proposed to

---

313 At the time of this writing, the currency exchange rate of the Euro to the Swedish Crown is 1 to 9.50. *See* the State Inquiry, (SOU 2000:20) *Steriliseringsfrågan i Sverige 1935–1975 Historisk belysning—Kartläggning—Intervjuer, ersättningen till tvångssteriliserade som infördes genom lagen* (1999:332) and its English summary.

314 *See* SOU 2011:61, *Vanvård i social barnavård Slutrapport*, p. 67 and its English summary.

315 *Lag* (2012:663) *om ersättning på grund av övergrepp eller försummelser i samhällsvården av barn och unga i vissa fall.*

316 For the history of this legislation, *see* Jameson Garland, ON SCIENCE, LAW, AND MEDICINE: THE CASE OF GENDER-"NORMALIZING" INTERVENTIONS ON CHILDREN DIAGNOSED AS DIFFERENT IN SEX DEVELOPMENT (Uppsala University 2016).

317 *See* Case 1968-12, judgment issued 19 December 2012. The Swedish Federation for Lesbian, Gay, Bisexual, Transgender and Queer Rights has driven this question for years, and initiated a damage claim on behalf of 160 plaintiffs to the Parliamentary Ombudsman, which was denied.

be damages in the amount of SEK 225,000 per individual, to be enacted as law by 2018.

### *1995 EU Membership and Swedish Discrimination Legislation*

The results of a ten-year evaluation of the 1979 Equal Treatment Act formed the bases for the 1991 Act Concerning Equal Treatment Between Women and Men at Work.[318] The 1991 Act kept much of the 1979 Equal Treatment Act, particularly its layout and enforcement mechanisms, however, the order was changed, beginning with the sections on the duty to take active measures, followed by the discrimination prohibition, then the third section still regarding enforcement and *JämO*. A very central aspect of the Swedish Model was kept, namely that central collective agreements could replace the Act's provisions on active equality measures. The burden of proof that plaintiff demonstrate that she was better objectively qualified was retained. A prohibition against harassment based on a refusal of sexual advances or a reporting of a sex discrimination claim was included. Several later amendments were made to the 1991 act, mostly those necessary to comply with Union law, including the EU shifting of the burden of proof.

Sweden became a EU member in 1995, entailing the obligation now of loyally implementing EU law. Sweden had been unofficially harmonizing its laws prior to its membership, such as with the 1991 Equal Treatment Act, but after 1995 harmonization no longer was optional. The European Convention finally was enacted as Swedish law in 1994, effective 1998, a requirement under dualism.[319] It was not enacted as a Swedish constitutional act, but given protection by Article 23 of the second chapter of the Instrument of Government prescribing that "[n]o act of law or other provision may be adopted which contravenes Sweden's undertakings under the European Convention." The flurry of EU directives addressing discrimination issues led to a corresponding flurry of legislative acts in Sweden. By 2006, Sweden had eleven legislative acts covering different grounds of discrimination in different settings:

- The 1991 Equal Treatment Act;
- The 1995 Parental Leave Act;
- The 1999 Measures to Counteract Ethnic Discrimination in Working Life Act;

---

318 *Jämställdhetslag* (1991:433).

319 *See* The Act on the European Convention on Human Rights and Fundamental Freedoms, *lag* (1994:1219) *om den europeiska konventionen angående skydd för de mänskliga rättigheterna och de grundläggande friheterna.*

- The 1999 Prohibition of Discrimination in Working Life of People with Disability Act;
- The 1999 Act Prohibiting Discrimination in Working Life based on Sexual Orientation;
- The 2001 Act on Equal Treatment of Students at Universities;
- The 2002 Act Prohibiting Discrimination on the Basis of Part-Time and Fixed-Term Work;
- The 2003 Act Prohibiting Discrimination with respect to Goods and Services;
- The 2006 Act Prohibiting Discrimination with respect to primary school children;
- A 2006 regulation as to anti-discriminatory terms in public procurement contracts;[320] and
- The 2006 Act on Genetic Integrity (prohibiting the use of genetic information against and individual).

The 2006 parliamentary committee charged with overhauling the discrimination legislation began by concluding that discrimination constitutes a violation of fundamental human rights and that legislation is one of several means of combating discrimination and thereby supporting these rights, citing the 1948 UNDHR, 1965 ICERD, 1966 ICCPR and ICESCR, 1979 CEDAW, 1989 CRC, Article 14 ECHR, ILO Discrimination (Employment and Occupation) Convention, 1958 (No. 111), as well as:

- That the European Union is founded on the principles of respect for human rights and fundamental freedoms as provided by Article 6.1 EU Treaty, and which according to Article 6.2, the Union is to respect fundamental rights as guaranteed by the European Convention;
- The case law of the European Court of Justice which has declared that human rights constitute an integral part of the general principles of law and should be safeguarded by the courts, and that the protection of human rights also embraces the rights contained in the European Convention;
- Article 13 EC Treaty, which empowers the Council, acting unanimously on a proposal from the Commission and following consultation with the European Parliament, to take appropriate action to combat discrimination based on sex, racial or ethnic origin, religion or belief, disability, age or sexual orientation; and

320 *Förordning* (SFS 2006:260) *om antidiskrimineringsvillkor i upphandlingskontrakt* was inspired at least partly by EO 11246.

- Article 21.1 EU Charter, which prohibits any discrimination based on any ground such as sex, race, color, ethnic or social origin, genetic features, language, religion or belief, political or any other opinion, membership of a national minority, property, birth, disability, age or sexual orientation.[321]

Finding that the regulatory situation in Sweden could at best be described as piecemeal, the committee proposed the introduction of a universal discrimination act.

### *The 2008 Discrimination Act*

A universal act was passed two years later, the 2008 Discrimination Act, which came into effect 1 January 2009.[322] The Act forbids unlawful discrimination on the basis of sex, transgender identity or expression, ethnicity,[323] religion or other belief, disability, sexual orientation or age.[324] Transgender identity or expression as well as age are new protected grounds under the Act. Three protections remain outside the act in separate acts, protections as to part-time and fixed-term workers, parental leave and the use of genetic information. The Act explicitly states that it is mandatory, and that any agreements in contravention of the rights or obligations afforded under the act are void.[325]

---

321 *See* SOU 2006:22 *En sammanhållen diskrimineringslagstiftning, del* 1 45.

322 *Diskrimineringslag* 2008:567. The 2008 Discrimination Action replaced eight of the discrimination acts listed above, with the exception of the 1995 Parental Leave Act, the 2002 Act Prohibiting Discrimination on the Basis of Part-Time and Fixed-Term Work, and the 2006 Act on Genetic Integrity, which are still separate acts. An English translation of the 2008 Discrimination Act is available Equality Ombudsman of Sweden website, do.se.

323 The Swedish legislator deliberately removed "race" from the list of protected grounds in the 2008 Discrimination Act. According to its legislative preparatory works, this was to demonstrate that a biological concept of race is unacceptable: "[T]here is no scientific basis for dividing human beings into different races and from a biological perspective, consequently is there neither any reason to use the word race with respect to human beings." The Parliament also stated that the Swedish Government in the international arena is to act so that the word "race" is avoided to as great a degree as possible in official international texts. The Government also was to review the extent to which the term "race" is included in Swedish laws not based on international texts, and as far as possible, suggest a different term. No such alternative term has been suggested to date, either by the Government or the Parliament.

324 Sweden received a three-year extension with respect to implementing Directive 2000/78, but failed to implement age protections by the extended deadline of 2006.

325 Labor law historically until EU membership in 1995 was the predominant approach, with the social partners regulating labor market issues through collective agreements and a general resistance by the social partners with respect to legislation, as seen with the

The protections in the Act encompass employment (both private and public), education, labor market policy, starting a business and professional recognition, membership in organizations such as labor unions, housing, the provision of goods and services both as provider and as customer, social benefits, social insurance and military service. Unlawful discrimination is defined as direct and indirect discrimination, harassment, sexual harassment and instructions to discriminate. Direct discrimination is where a person is treated less favorably than another is, has been or would have been treated in a comparable situation, provided that the difference in treatment is based on sex, sexual identity, ethnic background, religion or other religious belief, disability, sexual orientation or age. Indirect discrimination occurs with the application of a provision, criteria or procedure that appears neutral but is likely to disfavor someone of a particular sex, sexual identity, ethnic background, religion or other religious belief, disability, sexual orientation[326] or age, unless the provision, criteria or procedure can objectively be supported by a lawful objective and the means to achieve it are appropriate and necessary. The prohibition against harassment covers conduct related to sex, sexual identity, ethnic background, religion or other religious belief, disability, sexual orientation or age, and which violates the integrity of a person. Sexual harassment is behavior of a sexual nature that violates a person's integrity. Unlawful instructions to discriminate are orders or instructions to discriminate against a person given to someone in a position subordinate or dependent to the person giving the order or instruction or who, in relation to such a person, has undertaken to perform a task. Prohibitions against retaliatory measures as well as an obligation to investigate and implement measures against harassment are also included.

Active measures are the second prong of equality work in Sweden. The Act includes the obligation to conduct active measures, expanding them to cover not only issues relating to sex, ethnic background and religion or other

---

history of the first Equality Act. Employment legislation regulating the relationship between the individual and the employer historically was considered alien to the Swedish Model, and discrimination issues at the workplace are very much employment law issues. This collective model, strongly entrenched in the system anchored in the 1930's, has had difficulties dealing with the issues of discrimination, particularly structural discrimination. Even after concessions by the social partners as to the appropriateness of discrimination legislation, remnants of this attitude still remain, *see, e.g.*, Nycander 380 who argues that the inefficacy of the Swedish discrimination legislation is a result of trying to artificially impose a foreign system of legislation on the already well-functioning system of agreement between the social partners.

326 The Marriage Code was amended in 2009 from marriage only being between a man and a woman to being between two individuals regardless of sex.

religious beliefs, but also to sexual identity and age. Employers are to take active measures regarding recruitment, education and the development of skills, job seeking and applications. The employer is to prepare an annual equal treatment plan for work with active measures to achieve equal rights and opportunities in working life, regardless of sex, sexual identity, ethnic background, religion or other religious belief, disability, sexual orientation or age. This plan is to contain an overview of the active measures required at the workplace according to the Act together with a report of those measures the employer intends to commence or implement during the forthcoming year.

Remedies under the act can be damages (compensatory, nominal or discrimination damages) and the voiding of certain employment decisions. Damages can be reduced to zero if such is deemed fair.

### *The Discrimination Ombudsman*

*JämO* was established in 1980 after the "whole" 1979 Equal Treatment Act became effective. Five different Ombudsmen eventually were established under the different acts, *JämO* (1980), the Ombudsman against Ethnic Discrimination (1986), the Disability Ombudsman (1999), the Ombudsman against Discrimination because of Sexual Orientation (1999) and the Children's Ombudsman (1993). These first four were merged in 2009 into one authority, the Office of the Ombudsman against Discrimination ("DO") under the 2008 Act. DO is to work to eliminate discrimination in all areas of society, to promote equal rights and opportunities, equality between men and women and prevent and counteract racism, xenophobia and homophobia, provide advice and assist in ensuring that those exposed to discrimination can exercise their rights and information to the public and governmental authorities in general.

DO has the legislative mandate to pursue individual claims of discrimination, but has decided instead to focus mostly on education and public opinion formation. DO received 294 complaints of ethnic discrimination in 2013 and not one was pursued, with DO stating that the employers had "provided objective explanations for their actions and that it was difficult to determine whether any discrimination had occurred."[327] This can comparied to the fact

327 *See* the editorial, Eve Schömer, Lena Svenaeus and Lars Viklund, 'DO sviker diskriminerade', Svenska Dagbladet, 15 April 2014. Svenaeus was herself the Sex Equality Discrimination Ombudsman from 1994 to 2000. According to the statistics in the editorial, DO received almost 2000 complaints in 2012, 379 were dismissed without investigation, 21 were filed with the court and 27 were settled. After a missive from the Government about this poor performance, DO during 2013 received 1827 complaints and 887 were dismissed without any investigation.

that the Labour Court has only found two cases of unlawful discrimination on the basis of ethnicity since the passage of the 1986 Act.[328]

### *Access to Justice Issues in Sweden*

Sweden generally is a defendant-friendly legal forum with few concessions to access to justice issues. Amendments to pleadings are limited with complaints based on facts. There is limited discovery with the courts only having the sanction of fines for failures to produce documents. The original statute of limitations under the 1979 Equal Treatment Act was four months, extended to six months in 2008, and is still four months under the 1995 Parental Leave Act.

The Labour Court ("AD") is an independent, specialized court outside both the administrative and general court systems. A judging panel of the Labour Court typically consists of seven members, three non-partisan members who are the chair and vice-chair trained in law and a third member who is an expert in the labor market, as well as four partisan members, two chosen by the employer side, two by the employee side. If the case concerns a claim of discrimination, as of 2009 the judging panel is to comprise five members, of which only two are to represent the social partners. The parties to the case can request however the typical seven-member panel. Employment discrimination claims are either brought directly to the Labour Court by either the social partners or the Discrimination Ombudsman, and then the Labour Court is the first and final instance.[329] If an individual brings a claim of discrimination, the judgment can be appealed to the Labour Court.[330] The case law of the Labour Court demonstrates a consistency of result and approach as to issues of

328 *See* AD 2002 no. 128 *DO v. Service Companies Employers' Association and GfK Sverige Inc. in Lund* in which the Labour Court found that defendant had indirectly discriminated against plaintiff by applying a requirement of "clear" Swedish that was higher than necessary for the position and AD 2011 no. 13, *DO v. The City of Helsingborg* in which the Labour Court found that a manager had ethnically harassed an employee from eastern Europe by calling her an "East Girl" when she had asked him to stop doing so.

329 The Labour Court is outside both the administrative and general courts. The Labour Court does not fall directly within either of these two systems, as it is in itself a court of first and final instance.

330 The Swedish Supreme Court does not have final jurisdiction with respect to the decisions of the Labour Court. However, a right exists to petition the Swedish Supreme Court to vacate the Labour Court's final judgment if it is found to manifestly contradict the law and enter a judgment *de novo*, an argument seldom raised, *see* Chapter 58 § 1(4) of the Swedish Code of Judicial Procedure.

discrimination.[331] The first and only claim of indirect discrimination in which a plaintiff has prevailed was against Volvo for having a height requirement as to employment in 2005.[332] Approximately thirty cases of unlawful ethnic discrimination have been brought to the Labour Court, with it finding for the plaintiff in two.[333]

As to remedies, equity is not an institution in Swedish law, consequently the courts have no equitable powers, and cannot order for example, the hiring of an individual. A decision made by an employer with respect to existing employment can be voided, but the employer ultimately cannot be forced to effect the decision, such as take back a former employee, and can simply pay damages. Punitive damages are not awarded, only economic, nominal or discrimination damages. Economic damages are only awarded where the plaintiff already is an employee. Exemplary damages are awarded by the Labour Court in modest amounts, typically somewhere between SEK 25,000 and 50,000. The third category of damages, discrimination damages, were introduced by the 2008 Discrimination Act as enhanced damages so that employers would be deterred from discriminating. The Labour Court to date has awarded such in only

331 For an overview of the discrimination case law of the Swedish Labour Court, *see* Laura Carlson, *Addressing Unlawful Discrimination: The Swedish Journey*, in Laura Carlson, Örjan Edström and Birgitta Nyström (eds.), GLOBALIZATION, FRAGMENTATION, LABOUR AND EMPLOYMENT LAW: A SWEDISH PERSPECTIVE (Iustus 2016).

332 AD 2005 no. 87, *JämO v. The Association of Swedish Engineering Industrial Employers and Volvo Cars Inc. in Gothenburg.*

333 One not only has to take into account the Swedish labor law model, and legislation as at times gap-filling, but also the judicial and political systems when assessing the case law. The "hybrid" legal systems of the Nordic countries are characterized by self-regulation by central organizations, courts not perceiving their role as making law, but rather interpreting legislative intent, combined however with a fairly significant reliance on case law, earning them their own designation as the "Nordic legal family." Because of their perceived role as interpreters of the law, when faced with an issue not covered by the direct text of the statute, judges turn to the legislative preparatory works in order for the court theoretically to come as close to the intent of the legislator as possible. For a discussion as to the Nordic legal family, *see, e.g.*, Jaakko Husa, *Guarding the Constitutionality of Law in the Nordic Countries: A Comparative Perspective*, 48 AM.J.COMP.L. 345 (2000). With respect to the Nordic labor law model, *see* Niklas Bruun, *The Nordic Model for Trade Union Activity* in Niklas Bruun, Boel Flodgren, Marit Halvorsen, Hakan Hyden and Ruth Nielsen, THE NORDIC LABOUR RELATIONS MODEL LABOUR LAW AND TRADE UNIONS IN THE NORDIC COUNTRIES—TODAY AND TOMORROW 1 (Dartmouth 1992).

thirteen cases, with an average award of SEK 62,700.[334] To determine whether there truly is an enhance award of damages in these cases, a comparison can be made to the nominal damages awarded in the discrimination cases since the first 1979 Act. The average of nominal damages awarded for discrimination in the 1980's was SEK 19,000, the 1990's SEK 37,000, the 2000's SEK 51,600 and during the 2010's, SEK 61,923 (including both nominal and discrimination damages).[335] Adjusting for inflation, the average award of SEK 19,000 in 1980 is today worth SEK 59,983.[336] Taking the maximum average of discrimination damages at SEK 62,700, this entails that the amount of damages since the 1979 Act has materially increased by 4.5%, an increase that does not appear to reach the threshold of enhanced.

This increase in the amount of discrimination damages awarded of 4.5% can be contrasted against the increase during the same period of trial costs and fees. In Sweden, trial costs and fees are generally awarded according to the English rule, which means that the non-prevailing party pays the trial costs and fees for both parties.[337] The Labour Court can order that each party bear its own costs if the losing party had reasonable cause to have the dispute tried, but this is seldom invoked by the Court and even more rarely in cases where the employee has lost.[338] The amount of trial costs and fees as awarded by the Labour Court in discrimination cases demonstrates a trend that deviates radically from the relatively modest increases in the amount of damages, with trial costs and fees having increased by 170% since the 1980's. Consequently, during this 45-year time span in which the discrimination laws have been in place,

---

334 AD 2016 no. 38, AD 2015 no. 72, AD 2015 no. 51, AD 2015 no. 44, AD 2015 no. 12, AD 2014 no. 19, AD 2013 no. 71, AD 2013 no. 29, AD 2013 no. 18, AD 2011 no. 37, AD 2011 no. 23, AD 2011 no. 02 and AD 2010 no. 91.

335 For a listing of the cases upon which these statistics are based, *see* Carlson 156–8.

336 According to Statistics Sweden, SEK 1,000 in 1980 is worth SEK 3,157 in 2016 compensating for inflation, *see* scb.se.

337 Even if a party prevails on the legal merits, the Labour Court can reallocate the costs and fees depending upon the amount of the claims made. For example, in AD 2015 no. 44 plaintiff initially pled damages in the amount of SEK 100,000 and was only awarded SEK 25,000. The Labour Court found that plaintiff actually did not prevail due to this disparity and ordered plaintiff to pay defendant's litigation costs of SEK 42,300, resulting in a pyrrhic victory. In a similar case, AD 2013 no. 29, plaintiff pled damages of SEK 200,000 and was awarded discrimination damages of SEK 50,000, the same 25% ratio as in AD 2015 no. 44, but there was not ordered by the Court to pay the trial costs and fees of the losing party.

338 § 5(2) of the 1974 Labour Disputes (Judicial Procedure) Act, *see e.g.*, AD 1999 no. 51, AD 1996 no. 79 and AD 1991 no. 65.

the amount damages per plaintiff has increased by roughly 4.5% even after the implementation of enhanced discrimination damages, while the trial costs and fees have risen 170%.

This disparity renders the option of litigation even more expensive to already disadvantaged plaintiffs. The financial risks a plaintiff assumes if unsuccessful have successively increased due to the increase in costs and fees and the parallel relative stagnation of damage awards. During the 1980's, damages and fees were comparable, SEK 59,983 and SEK 71,139 in today's value. During the 2010's, this disparity is significantly greater, SEK 62,700 as against SEK 192,122. To this can be added the success rates of the different claims, with the lowest success rate for claims of ethnic discrimination; only two of over thirty such cases have been brought successfully by plaintiffs, a less than 7% chance of prevailing.

The trends with respect to damages and attorneys' costs and fees, combined with the low success rates, create a significant deterrent for plaintiffs bringing discrimination claims. Litigation is arguably not an affordable option for most discrimination plaintiffs. This is particularly true in light of the fact that it is often cases of discrimination with respect to hirings or firings, consequently individuals who are unemployed. The Discrimination Ombudsmen as well as labor unions can bring discrimination cases on behalf of plaintiffs, and have greater resources than individuals so that the financial risks associated with litigating discrimination claims are not as decisive. However, DO's policy has resulted in it pursuing very few cases. As to the labor unions, there is no duty of representation under Swedish labor law, so unions are basically free to decline to represent members in discrimination claims, and the only redress the union member/employee has is leaving the union.

There is a limited right to receive legal aid. An individual cannot have assets and yearly income of more than SEK 260,000 and there is a limit of one-hundred hours of legal advice. If the individual is a member of a labor union, the labor union is to be first contacted before legal aid. If an individual has legal assistance coverage in their home insurance, the insurance coverage is to be used instead.[339] A caveat here though is that most if not all insurance

339 Legal assistance generally under most home insurance policies is limited, with a range from SEK 75,000 to SEK 200,000 and often a deductible of 20%. Some policies also cover liability for the other party's fees for up to 80%. A contrasting development can be seen in the insurance offered employers. Municipalities can now purchase discrimination insurance with a deductible of SEK 35,000 and coverage up to SEK 500,000, with limits of SEK 200,000 for legal counsel and SEK 100,000 for employee claims, *see* P Jodenius, *Tingsryd försäkrar sig mot diskrimineringslagen*, SMÅLANDS POSTEN, 9 January 2015 and

policies exempt employment disputes, relying instead on the labor unions to pursue such claims. Given the financial risks for plaintiffs, many claimants have opted to take discrimination claims to small claims court, which has a ceiling as to damages of approximately SEK 22,000, with a filing fee of SEK 900 with a limited risk of liability as to paying the other party's trial costs and fees. Given this ceiling in damages, it is questionable whether small claims court is a suitable alternative from an access to justice perspective.

## Part 7: Institutional and Theoretical Frameworks

When embarking on a comparative discrimination law analysis, several aspects other than simply a comparison of legislation or cases need to be kept in mind. These include a conscious choice of a comparative law theory, and often a second theoretical approach in tangent,[340] such as Feminist, Critical Race, Post-Colonial, Queer or Intersectionality legal theories or overarching discrimination theories.[341] Other theories can also illuminate aspects in a discrimination law comparison, such as Law and economics, Law and Sociology, Critical Legal Studies, Law and Society and Post-modernism. In certain cases, a

---

Söderberg & Partners, *Försäkringsinformation—Tierps kommun for the period from 2015–2017*, available at the website of Tierp's municipality, tierp.se. The insurance solution for employers (potential wrongdoers having significantly greater financial resources) is considerably better than the insurance solutions offered employees, those who were harmed and having considerably fewer resources.

340 *See* David Oppenheimer, Sheila Foster and Sora Han, COMPARATIVE EQUALITY AND ANTI-DISCRIMINATION LAW: CASES, CODES, CONSTITUTIONS AND COMMENTARY (Univ. Casebook Series)(Foundation Press 2012).

341 *See e.g.*, Deborah Hellman and Sophia Moreau, THE PHILOSOPHICAL FOUNDATIONS OF DISCRIMINATION LAW (Oxford 2013). One example of a universal discrimination theory can be seen in Tarunabh Khaitan, A THEORY OF DISCRIMINATION LAW (Oxford 2015). Khaitan creates a general framework for a theoretical approach to discrimination law as a whole by answering three fundamental questions: Who is protected by discrimination law, who bears it duties and what are those duties? The general justifying aim of discrimination law "is to further the well-being of person by securing access to the basic goods to those who lack such access because of their affiliation to protected groups." Protected groups are those whose members suffer substantial, abiding and pervasive disadvantage. Khaitan's theory facilitates assessments as to whether new protection grounds are warranted. For another universal discrimination theory, *see* Iyiola Solanke, DISCRIMINATION AS STIGMA—A THEORY OF ANTI-DISCRIMINATION LAW (Hart 2017).

doctrinal (black letter law)[342] approach is sufficient to obtain valuable insight into a comparative law issue. Choices also have to be made with respect to the comparator countries, their internal industrial relations model if an employment discrimination issue, as well as the role of law in society and access to justice concerns. This part very briefly addresses these frameworks from the perspective of highlighting potential strengths and pitfalls when making a comparative discrimination law analysis.

### *Comparative Law Theories*

As a methodology, comparative law can be traced back at least to the Romans, a natural approach at a time of concurrent legal systems within the Empire. Canon law and European universities during the Middle Ages also served as points of unification and dissemination in the different local legal systems. Roman law was then used in many European countries as gap-filling, *ius commune*, with both direct and indirect receptions later into national legal systems. The idea of an *ius commune*, a common European law, is still very much alive in the European Union.[343] In federal systems today, such as the United States or Germany, comparative law is always an aspect of any lawyering, much as with the Romans, as differences must be determined and the applicable law identified. Adopting persuasive solutions from other legal systems within a federal system is common when facing legal issues lacking precedent in the jurisdiction at hand.

Modern comparative law theories and methods[344] are products of the combination of the rise of the nation state and the subsequent opportunity to compare the new national legal systems, as well of the new scientific and academic methods stemming from the Enlightenment. The International Association for Labour Legislation and its International Labour Office founded in Paris in 1900 are examples of early modern comparative law efforts. Modern comparative law[345] can be seen as having four objectives: resolving conflict of laws issues,

---

342 *See e.g.* Terry Hutchinson and Nigel Duncan, *Defining and Describing what we do: Doctrinal Legal Research*, 17(1) DEAKIN L. REV. 83–119 (2012).

343 *See e.g.*, Cees van Dam, EUROPEAN TORT LAW (2nd ed. Oxford 2013) and the chapter concerning *Ius Commune* at 127–164.

344 Geoffrey Samuel, *Does One Need an Understanding of Methodology in Law before One Can Understand Methodology in Comparative Law*, in Mark Van Hoecke (ed.), METHODOLOGIES OF LEGAL RESEARCH 177–208, 178 (Hart 2011).

345 For more on the topic of comparative law, *see e.g.*, Mauro Bussani and Ugo Mattei (eds.), THE CAMBRIDGE COMPANION TO COMPARATIVE LAW (Cambridge 2012); Peter de Cruz, COMPARATIVE LAW IN A CHANGING WORLD (3rd ed. Routledge 2006); Jaakko Husa, A NEW INTRODUCTION TO COMPARATIVE LAW (Bloomsbury 2015); Pierre

harmonizing legislation within national, supranational or transnational systems, improving legal knowledge and as a tool for shaping or guiding domestic decision-making.[346] Within each of these, the distinction can often be made between *de lege lata* and *de lege ferenda*, the current law and the law as it ought to be. The comparative component shapes the analysis as to the discussion of the law as it ought to be.

An additional challenge when comparing legal systems needs be mentioned, and that is language. Even where there is a common language, one must always be sensitive when comparing legal systems to the fact that even the same word or concept can have radically different meanings in different legal systems.[347] Four general methods of comparative law are briefly presented below, the functional, legal transplants, system and legal formants approaches, however, this list is not exhaustive.

The traditional functional comparative law approach focuses on identifying norms, then the social functions of those norms in order to evaluate the operation of the normative arrangements of the system.[348] This approach has been criticized for looking at only half the baby, simply the norms generated within the system as opposed to the norms as within their systems, the decision-making processes and the dynamics surrounding this environment. This approach then produces too little knowledge about the processes of legal systems,

---

Legrand and Roderick Munday (eds.), COMPARATIVE LEGAL STUDIES: TRADITIONS AND TRANSITIONS (Cambridge Univ. Press 2003); Mathias Reimann and Reinhard Zimmermann (eds.), THE OXFORD HANDBOOK OF COMPARATIVE LAW (Oxford Univ. Press 2006); Annelise Riles (ed.), RETHINKING THE MASTERS OF COMPARATIVE LAW (Hart 2001); Geoffrey Samuel, AN INTRODUCTION TO COMPARATIVE LAW THEORY AND METHOD (Hart 2014); Mathias Siems, COMPARATIVE LAW (LAW IN CONTEXT) (Cambridge 2014); Konrad Zweigert and Hein Kötz, AN INTRODUCTION TO COMPARATIVE LAW (3rd ed. Oxford Univ. Press 1998); and Esin Örücü and David Nelken (eds.), COMPARATIVE LAW—A HANDBOOK (Hart 2007).

346 David J. Gerber, *System Dynamics: Toward a Language of Comparative Law?*, 46 AM. J. COMP. L. 719. 722, (1998) *citing* Eric Stein, *Uses, Misuses—And Nonuses of Comparative Law*, 72 NW. U. L. REV. 198 (1977).

347 *E.g.*, "dispositive" in English can mean affecting a settlement. In Swedish, "dispositive" with respect to law means that the law is gap-filling and not obligatory. *See generally* for more information on translation and comparative law, Simone Glanert, COMPARATIVE LAW—ENGAGING TRANSLATION (Routledge 2014).

348 *See* Jaakko Husa, *Functional Method in Comparative Law—Much Ado About Nothing?* 2(1) EPLJ 4–21 (2013) *citing* Ernst Rabel, GESAMMELTE AUFSÄTZE BAND III ARBEITEN ZUR RECHTSVERGLEICHUNG UND ZUR RECHTSVEREINHEITLICHUNG 180–234 (Tübingen 1967). *See also* Michele Graziadei, *The Functionalist Heritage*, in Legrand 100–127, and Ralf Michaels, *The Functionalist Method of Comparative Law*, in Reimann 339–382.

focusing instead on the "artifacts they produce."[349] Modern scholars have extended the object of a functional comparative law study in part as a response to this criticism, from simply a comparison of isolated provisions to a comparison of specific solutions for practically identical situations as achieved within legal systems through law:

> The point of departure for comparison ought to be, therefore, not the written rule of statutory law (or a precedent of court) but the sociolegal function. This point of departure is needed in order to avoid (or an attempt to avoid) the problem that one perceives the foreign systems mainly through the mind-set of one's own legal system. A solution to legal problems can be provided by a custom or by some other social practice not necessarily in an identifiable legal form.[350]

Zweigert and Kötz envisioned the functional comparative law method as comprising the following steps:

1. Posing a functional question (how is socio-legal problem X solved);
2. Presenting the systems and their way of solving problem X;
3. Listing the similarities and differences in ways of solving X;
4. Adopting a new point of view from which to consider explanations of differences and similarities; and
5. Evaluating critically and weighing any discoveries discerned.[351]

When different countries meet the same needs in different ways, the compelling question under the functional comparative law method then becomes why.

The legal transplant approach[352] with respect to legal borrowings from system to system is a much-debated reality. As seen above, international concepts of human rights, such as the ILO conventions, are brought into national systems. National systems, as seen for example in the Swedish context of contemplating discrimination legislation looking at the American experience, look to

349 Gerber 724.

350 Husa 12.

351 Husa 14 *citing* Zweigert and Kötz 44. *See also* Antonios Emmanuel Platsas, *The Functional and Dysfunctional in the Comparative Method of Law: Some Critical Remarks*, ELECTRONIC J. OF COMP. L. 12 (2008).

352 *See* Alan Watson, *Legal Transplants and Law Reform*, 92 L. QUART. REV. 79 (1976) and Watson, LEGAL TRANSPLANTS—AN APPROACH TO COMPARATIVE LAW (Georgia 1993).

other national systems with respect to solutions for legal problems: "[T]he reception of a foreign legal institution is not a matter of nationality, but a matter of usefulness and need. No one bothers to fetch a thing from afar when one has one as good or better at home, but only a fool would refuse a good medicine just because it did not grow in his own back garden."[353] One of the criticisms raised against legal transplants is the tendency to borrow without taking into consideration the conditions of the receiving legal system. Others argue that legal transplants in reality do not exist, for as soon as they are received by the new legal system, they immediately are changed by the new surroundings.[354]

A system approach to comparative law has as its object capturing and representing influences as to legal decision-making by looking at four principle sources: texts, institutions, decision-making communities and patterns of thought, discourses. An objective is to "reveal patterns in the ways that texts operate in legal systems—how they influence decisions and are influenced by those decisions."[355] This examination of texts naturally leads to the examination of the institutions in which decision-makers function. The third component places the decision-makers and the institutions within their broader communities. Finally, the patterns of thought, or discourses, are compared as deciphered from the interaction of these three components.[356]

The last comparative law method addressed here is legal formants. After assessing basically the same components as set out in the system approach, the scholar eliminates the complications and arrives at one legal rule, defined as a legal formant.[357] However, as legal systems are not the congruent systems desired, they can have conflicting or even contradictory legal formants. Comparisons of legal formants from different legal systems highlights

353 *See* George Mousourakis, *Legal Transplants and Legal Development: A Jurisprudential and Comparative Law Approach*, 54 ACTA JUR. HNG. 219, 224 (2013) *citing* Rudolf Jhering, GEIST DES RÖMISCHEN RECHTS I 8 (9th ed. 1955).

354 Pierre Legrand, *The Impossibility of Legal Transplants*, 4 MAASTRICHT J. OF EUR. AND COMP. L. 116–120 (1997).

355 Gerber 730.

356 The legal culture approach is similar, defined as the interplay of all four levels of the legal phenomena: the law in the books, the institutional infrastructure (judicial system and legal profession), patterns of legally relevant behaviour (*e.g.* legal transactions) and legal consciousness, *see* Erhard Blankenburg and Freek Bruinsma, DUTCH LEGAL CULTURE (Utrecht 1994).

357 Rodolfo Sacco, *Legal Formants: A Dynamic Approach to Comparative Law (Installment I of II)*, 39(1) AM. J. COMP. L. 1, 22 (1991); and Sacco, *Legal Formants: A Dynamic Approach to Comparative Law (Installment II of II)*, 39(2) AM. J. COMP. L. 343–402 (1991).

inconsistencies within legal systems, enriching the knowledge of the law generally.[358]

### *Legal Families, Styles and Traditions*

As a part of the academic endeavor of comparative law, certain modern comparative law scholars have classified legal systems into legal families or traditions.[359] Zweigert and Kötz[360] classified national legal systems into eight groups or families: Romanistic, Germanic, English, Nordic, Socialist, Far Eastern, Islamic and Hindu, based on the following criteria:

1. The historical background and development of a particular system;
2. Its predominant and characteristic mode of legal thinking;
3. Its distinctive legal institutions;
4. The hierarchy and interpretation of its legal sources; and
5. The ideological background of the system.

Another classification system is based on certain model, "core" systems. Legal rules and institutional structures are directly transplanted by conquest or colonization, or voluntarily adopted, such was the case with the Japanese modelling of law based on the German legal system. Seven core systems are identified: the French, German, Scandinavian, English, Russian, Islamic and Hindu. The crucial criterion for this classification of legal systems is the substantive content of laws, requiring attention to originality, derivation, and common elements, rather than to external factors.[361]

Caution must be used, however, when classifying legal systems. Such categorizations, to be useful, must be invoked critically as a tool, and not as a crutch.[362] A further complication is mixed legal systems, such as certain African countries, where state European-colonial legal systems exist parallel to tribal and religious legal systems, defying any simple categorization.

---

358 *See also* Sacco, *Legal Formants I* 6 as to comparing socialist and non-socialist legal systems.

359 For more information on different legal traditions, *see* Patrick Glenn, LEGAL TRADITIONS OF THE WORLD: SUSTAINABLE DIVERSITY IN LAW (5th ed. Oxford 2014).

360 Zweigert and Kötz 68–75.

361 *See* George Mousourakis, *Legal Transplants and Legal Development: A Jurisprudential and Comparative Law Approach*, 54 ACTA JUR. HNG. 219, 225 (2013) *citing* Pierre Arminjon, Boris Nolde and Martin Wolff, TRAITE DE DROIT COMPARE, VOL. 1 47 (Paris, 1950).

362 *See* Jaako Husa, *Classification of Legal Families Today—Is it time for a memorial hymn?* 56(1) Revue internationale de droit comparé 11–38 (2004).

### *Comparative Labor and Discrimination Law*

The modern legal treatment of issues of discrimination began with the institution of slavery as seen in the parts above, and bled out into issues of labor both internationally and nationally, issues of emancipation for slaves, workers and women. When assessing questions of discrimination as related to employment from a comparative law perspective, it is imperative to also take into consideration the legal models of industrial relations existing in the comparator countries. Otto Kahn-Freund, the pioneer in the field of comparative labor law, raised the question of the limits of comparisons to, and more importantly borrowing from, foreign legal systems outside their context in the 1970's when the UK was on the verge of EU membership. In his famous words:

> The use of the comparative method requires a knowledge not only of the foreign law, but also of its social, and above all its political context. The use of comparative law for practical purposes becomes an abuse only if it is informed by a legalistic spirit which ignores this context of the law.[363]

A first characteristic of different industrial relations models is whether they are tripartite (involving the state and the social partners in the form of employers and employee organizations), bipartite (typically involving the social partners), or neither with respect to achieving legally-binding solutions as to labor market issues. All three national systems addressed in this work are tripartite, but with different balances. The Swedish system has the least amount of participation by the state in the form of legislation, with many of the terms of employment set out by collective agreement, typical of the Nordic models with the strong emphasis of self-regulation by the social partners. The UK is heavy on national statutory regulation, and the US has a more individual contract-based approach to employment conditions. Another model not addressed in this work due to lack of space, but central is the German Works Council model that has been adopted by the EU.

Social security also plays an important role in these models, strengthening the position of the employees and lessening the power of employers in those systems providing strong social protection, such as pensions, sickness insurance, parental leave, occupational hazards and vacations. Where labor unions provide such benefits, union membership is central to securing social security

---

363 Otto Kahn-Freund, *On Uses and Misuses of Comparative Law*, 37 MOD. L. REV. 1, 27 (1974).

benefits, and unions become quasi-state actors. Where the state provides social security, the state becomes a necessary partner to employees and employers.[364]

Comparative discrimination law in contrast covers the entire span of human existence, issues of slavery, labor, citizenship, religion, housing, social welfare, family and reproduction, to name a few. To avoid such discrimination protections from being simply "empty" words, any analysis of the issues necessitates addressing access to justice aspects.[365] Many countries have discrimination protections, a key question is whether the necessary legal mechanisms are in place for plaintiffs to be able to successfully make claims. Additional layers in comparative discrimination law are the societal structures and bias existing in the system, both of which require analyses outside of black letter of the law to understand and counteract. The Outcrit legal theories discussed below begin to address this complexity.

### *Role of Law*

A vital component in any comparative legal analysis is assessing the national legal system's perception of the role of law. For example, American and British abolitionists used the law and the courts as vehicles for societal change already in the 18th century. In contrast, the emphasis for social change in Sweden has not been through the law or the courts, but rather by affecting public opinion and through the provision of social welfare. One can discuss this distinction as between legal justice and social justice, or as between liberal and communitarian perspectives of the law. A summary of major differences between liberal (bourgeois) rights and communitarian (socialist) rights can be envisioned as follows:

364 *See also* for the inclusion of national culture, Boyd Black, *Comparative Industrial Relations Theory: The Role of National Culture*, 16(7) THE INT'L. J. OF HUMAN RESOURCE MANAGEMENT 1137–1158 (2005).

365 *See generally* David Oppenheimer, Sheila Foster and Sora Han, COMPARATIVE EQUALITY AND ANTI-DISCRIMINATION LAW: CASES, CODES, CONSTITUTIONS AND COMMENTARY (UNIVERSITY CASEBOOK SERIES)(Foundation Press 2012). *See also* Sandra Fredman, DISCRIMINATION LAW (2nd ed. Oxford 2011).

TABLE 1 *Liberal and communitarian rights compared*[a]

| Liberal rights | Communitarian rights |
|---|---|
| – Rights are entitlements | – Rights are policy pronouncements |
| – Rights are ends | – Rights are the means to an end |
| – Rights are political | – Rights are organizational |
| – Rights are negative | – Rights are positive |
| – Rights depend on the activation of the right holder | – Rights do not depend on the activation of the right holder |
| – Rights protect individuals against the attacks of others | – Rights advance harmonious communal life |
| – Rights are conditional on the right-holders fulfilling their own obligations | – Rights are dependent on others fulfilling their correlative obligations |
| – Rights are related to a supporting set of sanctions | – Rights relate to mandatory rules but not supporting sanctions |
| – Rights are (or seek to be clearly) defined | – Rights are intentionally vague |
| – The exercise of rights and violation are private affairs | – Rights are public affairs |
| – Rights are not economic | – Rights are largely economic |
| – Rights are "legalistic" and individualistic | – Rights are not individualistic nor legalistic |

a Tom Campbell, *The Left and the Rights: A Conceptual Analysis of the Idea of Socialist Rights and Markovits*, 45 U. CHIC. L. R. 612 (1978). *See also* N.E. Simmonds, *Rights Socialism and Liberalism*, 5 LEGAL STUDIES 1 (1985).

This communitarian approach can be seen as stemming from socialist legal theory as ultimately derived from the writings of Karl Marx. Marx argued that law was a vehicle of class oppression and that following the proletarian revolution, the bourgeois State would be swept aside and replaced by a dictatorship of the proletariat, and society would have no further need of laws.[366] The Soviet Jurist Evgeny Pashukanis framed this premise somewhat differently in a "commodity exchange" theory of the law, in that the law protects the rights of individuals in a contractual relationship. In a communist society, the law

366 Karl Marx, *The Critique of the Gotha Programme (1875)* in Karl Marx and Friedrich Engels, SELECTED WORKS, VOLUME THREE 13–30 (Progress Publishers Moscow 1970).

eventually would disappear to be replaced by administration.[367] Many socialist legal systems today tend towards this communitarian approach as to the law and discrimination protections.[368] A similar question that can be raised is the role of the constitution in the legal system, whether it can be cited by individuals in claims for rights with remedies, or whether it is to be viewed instead simply as guidance for lawmakers.

### *Access to Justice*

A topic related to the role of law in society is access to justice. Legal systems that envision the law as a tool of societal change address access to justice issues more explicitly, as they must, compared to legal systems in which societal change is to occur outside the legal system. Access to justice comprises several elements, among which can be included fair and public hearings before independent and impartial tribunals, legal aid, the right to legal counsel and the right to an effective remedy.[369] Judicial procedural rules are also imperative in questions of access to justice, including the length of the statute of limitations, with shorter periods barring the bringing of cases. Other significant rules include whether pleadings must initially be based on fact, or can be based on belief later to be amended by fact, whether they can be amended at all, as well as whether recordkeeping requirements exist, and the strength of discovery mechanisms during litigation, particularly with respect to obtaining information from employers. As to legal counsel, legal aid, pro bono systems, contingent fees, fee shifting and class actions all affect access to justice. The burden of proof has been seen as central here both by the US and the EU, with the EU discrimination directives shifting the burden of proof in a manner similar to that in the United States.

Access to justice is an integral component with respect to discrimination protection as discriminations claims are brought by individuals who often do not have the financial resources to do so. Legal discrimination protections can be quite similar across legal systems and appear equally strong, while

---

367 R. Warrington, *Pashukanis and the Commodity Form Theory*, 9(1) INT'L. J. OF THE SOCIOLOGY OF LAW 1–22 (1981). *See, e.g.*, Kevät Nousiainen, *Transformative Nordic Welfare: Liberal and Communitarian Trends in Family and Market Law*, in Kevät Nousiainen (ed.), RESPONSIBLE SELVES—WOMEN IN THE NORDIC LEGAL CULTURE (Ashgate 2001).

368 *See e.g.*, Barbara Havelkova, GENDER EQUALITY IN LAW: UNCOVERING THE LEGACIES OF CZECH STATE SOCIALISM (Hart 2017).

369 *See* FRA and COE, HANDBOOK ON EUROPEAN LAW RELATING TO ACCESS TO JUSTICE (FRA and COE 2016).

differences in access to justice aspects can result in one system having true recourse for individuals and another system having in essence no recourse at all.

### *Legal Theories Addressing Different Protected Grounds*

Only a few of the legal theories addressing different protected grounds are taken up briefly below, the critical outsider theories ("Outcrit") of Critical Race, Post-Colonial, Feminist, Queer and Intersectionality legal theories.[370] Each of these Outcrit theories shares the basic premise of treating individuals as the subjects of the theory as opposed to theoretical objects.

Emancipation, equality and self-identity have been components driving these theories forward. They are methodological tools by which the nature of the legal discourse and its underlying assumptions are illuminated. Recognizing and legitimating the experiences of the individual are seen by these theories as steps towards coming to terms with the historical treatment of certain groups, finding atonement, reparation, resolution, as well as creating tools for combating existing discrimination.

#### Critical Race Theory

Critical Race Theory ("CRT" or Race Crits) emerged as a new strategy for dealing with the post-civil rights racial structure in the United States.[371] Issues of race followed slavery, taken up by the abolitionists, then by the struggles for equality and the removal of the badges of slavery after the Civil War. Despite almost a century of legislation and case law, many felt that the gains made up to the 1960's civil-rights era had been stymied and even rolled back. New, more nuanced approaches were necessary in order to combat the existing types of subtle, unconscious, or institutional racism that were more deeply entrenched

---

370 *See generally*, Margaret Davies, ASKING THE LAW QUESTION: THE DISSOLUTION OF LEGAL THEORY (4th ed. Sydney, 2017) and Raymond Wacks, UNDERSTANDING JURISPRUDENCE—AN INTRODUCTION TO LEGAL THEORY (4th ed. Oxford 2015).

371 For more on the history of the movement, *see* Kimberlé Crenshaw *et al.*, INTRODUCTION TO CRITICAL RACE THEORY: THE KEY WRITINGS THAT FORMED THE MOVEMENT (3rd ed. 1996); Crenshaw, *The First Decade: Critical Reflections, or "A Foot in the Closing Door"* in Francisco Valdes, Angela Harris, Jerome Mccristal Culp (eds.), CROSSROADS, DIRECTIONS, AND A NEW CRITICAL RACE THEORY (Temple 2002); and Athena D. Mutua, *The Rise, Development and Future Direction of Critical Race Theory and Related Scholarship*, 84 Denv. U. L. Rev. 329 (2006). For an annotated bibliography of CRT up to 1993, *see* Richard Delgado and Jean Stefancic, *Critical Race Theory: An Annotated Bibliography*, 79 VIRGINIA L. REV. 461 (1993).

and difficult to combat than the former overt varieties.[372] The still discriminatory structures of law and society were maintained by a colorblind liberal ideology that hid and protected white privilege, masking racism within the rhetoric of meritocracy and fairness. CRT emerged as a framework aimed at undermining this colorblind ideology through a deconstruction of its racist premises.[373]

The inception of CRT is traced back to Derrick Bell's 1980 article, *Brown v. Board of Education and the Interest Convergence Dilemma*.[374] Bell argued that *Brown* was not decided in favor of African-Americans because of true desire to achieve equality, but rather because of a fortuitous combination of material and sociopolitical circumstances he termed "interest convergence."[375] Bell pointed out that the National Association for the Advancement of Colored Persons ("NAACP") Legal Defense and Education Fund had been litigating school desegregation cases decades and achieving, at most, narrow victories. That the Supreme Court suddenly in a unanimous decision in 1954 appeared to grant the NAACP everything it had been working towards for decades was not logical. Bell set out three alternative reasons for the *Brown* decision: America's need to protect its reputation internationally,[376] the need for African-Americans to feel that progress could occur at home,[377] and the need for the South to be transformed from a rural poor economy to a productive one. These three reasons, the true driving forces behind *Brown*, were illustrative of what Bell termed

372 See Richard Delgado, *Liberal McCarthyism and the Origins of Critical Race Theory*, 94 IOWA L. REV. 1505, 1511 (2009).

373 Maria C. Malagon, Lindsay Perez Huber, Veronica N. Velez, *Our Experiences, Our Methods: Using Grounded Theory to Inform a Critical Race Theory Methodology*, 8 SEA.J.SOC.JUS. 253 (2009).

374 Derrick Bell, *Brown v. Board of Education and the Interest Convergence Dilemma*, 93 HARV. L. REV. 518 (1980).

375 Delgado (2009) 1507.

376 Time magazine, for example, wrote that "[i]n many countries, where U.S. prestige and leadership have been damaged by the fact of U.S. segregation, it will come as a timely reassertion of the basic American principle that 'all men are created equal';" *see* Bell 524.

377 Bell observed that Brown "offered much needed reassurance to American blacks that the precepts of equality and freedom so heralded during World War II might yet be given meaning at home. Returning black veterans faced not only continuing discrimination, but also violent attacks in the South which rivaled those that took place at the conclusion of World War I." This disillusionment and anger were poignantly expressed by one black actor, Paul Robeson, who in 1949 declared: "It is unthinkable ... that American Negroes would go to war on behalf of those who have oppressed us for generations ... against a country such as the Soviet Union which in one generation has raised our people to the full human dignity of mankind," *see id.* 525.

"interest convergence" in that the interests of the majority converged with the interests of the minority, consequently leading to the decision, in contrast to any true desire for equal rights.

Within the CRT framework, the term "race" in no way refers to any biological understanding, but rather is a social construct similar to gender: "Race is not ... simply a matter of physical appearance and ancestry.... [I]t is primarily a function of the meaning given to these."[378] Race as a social construct is summarized by one scholar:

> As a result, I start with the assumption that race and the "one drop of blood" rule are not based on any established scientific or biological definition. Of course, that does not mean race has no meaning or power in our society. Quite the contrary, race is an intractable force in American society touching every facet of day-to-day American life—often affecting where one goes to school, the job opportunities presented, who one marries, where one lives, the health care one receives, and even where one is interred following death. Race, in other words, continues to matter in our society, whether its definitional base is scientific or not. In fact, race has become a more powerful factor in American society because of its social construction. In sum, race, albeit socially constructed, continues to matter dearly in American society.[379]

As race is a social construct, groups of individuals who are not necessarily of the same ethnic origins can be "racialized." Race then is used as a verb to convey the notion that racialization or using race and its attendant meanings as part of a system of assignment is an active and intentional process.[380] Groups that have experienced such racialization include Native Americans, Asians,

---

378 *See* Ian F. Haney López, WHITE BY LAW (NYU Press 1996, 10th anniv. ed. 2006).

379 *See* Alex M. Johnson, Jr., *The Re-emergence of Race as a Biological Category: The Societal Implications-Reaffirmation of Race*, 94 IOWA L. REV. 1547, 1561 (2009) and Howard Winant, *Racial Dualism at Century's End* in Wahneema Lubiano (ed.), THE HOUSE THAT RACE BUILT 87, 89–90 (Knopf 1997).

380 *See, e.g.*, john a. powell, *A Minority-Majority Nation: Racing the Population in the Twenty-First Century*, 29 FORDHAM URB. L. J. 1395, 1415 (2002): "Race is the vehicle through which we can include or exclude; stratify or equalize; divide or combine.... [R]ace is a verb"; and Kendall Thomas, *The Eclipse of Reason: A Rhetorical Reading of Bowers v. Hardwick*, 79 VA. L. REV. 1805, 1806 (1993): "[R]ace is a verb ... we are 'raced' through a constellation of practices that construct and control racial subjectivities."

Muslims and Arabs.[381] According to CRT, racism is normalized, and over time, those living in it become inured.[382] Formal equality and legal rules requiring the equal treatment of blacks and whites are only capable of redressing the most dramatic forms of injustice, not the more routine forms suffered on a daily basis targeting persons of color.

CRT as a school of legal theory is not fixed but fluid, and purposefully so. Much as with Critical Legal Studies, this lack of a fixed content is perceived by CRT scholars mostly as a strength, and less often as a weakness, leading to both internal and external criticism.[383] Though lacking any one dominant legal theoretical approach, certain issues are deemed to be integral to CRT and can be condensed into five basic categories:[384]

1. Challenging the dominant race-neutral ideologies such as meritocracy and colorblindness that have contributed to deficient thinking about People of Color;
2. The intersectionality of race and racism with other forms of subordination, such as gender, class, sexuality and language, as structural and institutional factors influencing the everyday experiences of People of Color;
3. The centrality of experiential knowledge: The lived experiences of People of Color are instrumental in helping to understand how, and to what extent, race and racism mediate everyday life. People of Color are seen as creators of knowledge with a deeply-rooted sensibility to name racist injuries and identify their origins. CRT makes the explicit attempt to employ methodologies that center and capture the lived experiences of People of Color;

---

381 For discussions of the racialization of Asian-Americans and Arab-Americans as foreign, *see* Thomas W. Joo, *Presumed Disloyal: Executive Power, Judicial Deference and the Construction of Race Before and After September 11*, 34 COLUM. HUM. RTS. L. REV. 1 (2002) ("racialized presumptions of 'Oriental' foreignness and disloyalty ... have consistently influenced Asian American legal history"); Leti Volpp, *The Citizen and the Terrorist*, 49 U.C.L.A. L. REV. 1575 (2002); and Adrien Katherine Wing, *Civil Rights in the Post 911 World: Critical Race Praxis, Coalition Building, and the War on Terrorism*, 63 LA. L. REV. 717 (2003) (arguing that although "Arabs and Muslims are often stereotyped as dangerous, evil, sneaky, primitive, and untrustworthy, much as Blacks are, the criminality has a twist--they are considered potential or actual terrorists").

382 *See generally* Richard Delgado and Jean Stefancic (eds.), CRITICAL RACE THEORY: THE CUTTING EDGE (2nd ed. 2000); and Delgado and Stefancic, CRITICAL RACE THEORY: AN INTRODUCTION (NYU Press 2001).

383 *See e.g.* Edward L. Rubin, *Jews, Truth and Critical Race Theory*, 93 NW. U. L. REV. 525 (1999).

384 Malagon 256–7.

4. The transdisciplinary perspective invoking knowledge and methodological bases from ethnic studies, women's studies, sociology, history, and the law in constructing CRT's theoretical premise. These methodologies are used in the attempt to capture and understand better the experiences of marginalized communities over more traditional research methods; and.
5. The commitment to an anti-racist social justice agenda: CRT seeks to eliminate racism and other forms of subordination, empowering participants through research processes and developing reciprocity with the communities that are a part of their research.

CRT's initial focus was on the experience of African-Americans, the badges and inheritance of slavery that divided the population into a dominant, privileged majority and a subordinated, disadvantaged minority.[385] CRT spin-off theories broadened this focus to other minority groups as well as religious affiliations. For example, LatCrits and Asian American legal scholarship began to bring issues relating to religion more to the fore.[386] The terrorist bombings of the World Trade Center in 2001 and the subsequent backlash against persons of Arab or Muslim descent sealed the urgency of such inclusion:

> In the post-9/11 era, what exactly is meant by race? Race is composed significantly of a religious dimension that has not been critically isolated, analyzed or discussed. Islamic religious difference has been racialized in the context of the war on terror, just as religious differences contributed to the consolidation of Japanese American racial difference during World War II. Yet the existing architecture of domestic and international anti-discrimination law has avoided recognizing racial discrimination based on religious group difference. Domestic and international law simultaneously creates and obscures current "Muslim" racial identity. The most overt and publicly debated of law's methods in this regard is so-called racial profiling. Equally critical, however, is the incompleteness of legal remedies available to those targeted by religiously driven racial discrimination. Thus by both its commissions and omissions, law is implicated in this process of religioning race.[387]

---

385 *Compare* Forrest Wood, THE ARROGANCE OF FAITH: CHRISTIANITY AND RACE IN AMERICA FROM THE COLONIAL ERA TO THE TWENTIETH CENTURY (Knopf 1990).

386 *See e.g.*, Verna Sánchez, *Looking Upward and Inward; Religion and Critical Theory*, 19 CHICANO-LATINA L. REV. 431 (1998).

387 Margaret Chon and Donna E. Arzt, *Walking While Muslim*, 68 LAW & CONTEMP. PROBS. 215–7 (2005): "Walking While Muslim" is a play on the term popularized in the context of

The racialization of religion is now an established arena for CRT. A contrast can be drawn here to Europe historically, where religion has been a palpable driving factor of oppression, beginning with the Reformation, with social fault lines and the mechanisms of oppression often defined in religious terms.[388] Less palpable has been the endemic discrimination in Europe of certain ethnic groups, for example, the Jews, the Romani and in the Nordic countries, the Sami.[389]

"Post-racialism" reflects a belief that due to the significant racial progress that has been made, the state need no longer engage in race-based decision-making or adopt race-based remedies.[390] The argument is that the word "race" should no longer be used as it is outdated and no longer valid in today's world.[391] This can be seen from Chief Justice John Roberts' statement in *Parents Involved in Community Schools v. Seattle School District No. 1*, that "the way 'to achieve a system of determining admission to the public schools on a nonracial basis' is to stop assigning students on a racial basis. The way to stop discrimination on the basis of race is to stop discriminating on the basis of race."[392] That same year, the Swedish legislator removed the term "race" from the proposed discrimination legislation. As Professor john powell notes, post-race statements espouse a "false universalism"—a belief that every person is equal and requires no state-provided advantage. If society is post-race, then race-based remedies are undesirable as a lingering remnant of less enlightened times. Affirmative action programs or other race-conscious remedies are, by definition, inconsistent with a post-racial "reality." Although post-racialism may be a panacea for those with racial fatigue, it also evinces a type of racial amnesia—a desire to

---

African-American racial profiling, "Driving While Black." Both suggest that certain individuals are being targeted for no legitimate purpose.

388 *See* Edward L. Rubin, *Jews, Truth and Critical Race Theory*, 93 NW. U. L. REV. 525, 531 (1999).

389 *See* Mathias Möschel, LAW, LAWYERS AND RACE: CRITICAL RACE THEORY FROM THE UNITED STATES TO EUROPE (Routledge 2014), *see also* Möschel, *Race in mainland European legal analysis: towards a European critical race theory*, 34 (10) ETHNIC AND RACIAL STUDIES 1648–64 (2011) and Namita Chakrabarty, CRITICAL RACE THEORY IN ENGLAND (Routledge 2014).

390 *See* Sumi Cho, *Post-Racialism*, 94 Iowa L. Rev. 1589 (2009).

391 *See* Mario Barnes, *A Post-Race Equal Protection?* 98 Geo.L.J. 967, 970–1 (2010). *See also* Symposium, *Beyond the Final Frontier: A "Post-Racial" America?*, 25 HARV. BLACKLETTER L.J. 1 (2009); Ian F. Haney López, *Post-racial Racism: Racial Stratification and Mass Incarceration in the Age of Obama*, 98(3) Cal. L. Rev. 1023 (2010).

392 *See Parents Involved in Community Schools v. Seattle School District No. 1*, 551 U.S. 701, 741 (2007).

forget that those marked by race neither asked for the designation nor can they escape its present day meanings and effects.[393]

### Postcolonial Legal Theory

Issues of racism also began to be viewed through the lenses of imperialism, colonialism, decolonialism and neo-colonialism: "[P]ostcolonialism is now the main mode in which the West's relation to its 'other' is critically been explored, and law has been … [in] the forefront of that very relation."[394] Postcolonialism provides an innovative method for thinking about existing structures of law, provoking a different reading outside the Eurocentric enterprise. As with Critical Race, there is little agreement between postcolonial scholars as to the precise nature and scope of this theory.[395]

Postcolonial legal theorists focus on the role of law as played during the colonial processes, the superimposition of laws, values and norms, mostly Western, on annexed cultures starting from the 15th century colonization as to much of the non-European world, up until WWII.[396] The "Other" is a key concept on a binary that is often European/non-European, similar to that of Critical Race's black/white. The Other often were simply subordinated objects, even property. This superimposition of Western values as well as objectification of the Other is argued as a continuing legacy of colonialism to the present date.[397]

---

393 Barnes 970–1.

394 *See* Alpana Roy, *Postcolonial Theory and Law: A Critical Introduction*, 29(2) ADELAIDE L. REV. 315–357, 315 (2008) *citing* Peter Fitzpatrick and Eve Darian-Smith, *Laws of the Postcolonial: an Insistent Introduction* in Fitzpatrick and Darian-Smith (eds.), LAWS OF THE POSTCOLONIAL 1–15, 4 (1999). *See generally* Margaret Davies, *Race and Colonialism: Legal Theory as 'White Mythology* in Davies, ASKING THE LAW QUESTION.

395 Roy 316.

396 *See e.g.*, Leela Gandhi, POST-COLONIAL THEORY (Columbia Univ. Press 1998); Dipesh Chakrabarty, PROVINCIALIZING EUROPE: POST-COLONIAL THOUGHT AND HISTORICAL DIFFERENCE (Princeton Univ. Press 2000); Chandra Talpade Mohanty, FEMINISM WITHOUT BORDERS: DECOLONIZING THEORY, PRACTICING SOLIDARITY (Duke Univ. Press 2003); Piyal Haldar Law, ORIENTALISM AND POSTCOLONIALISM: JURISDICTION OF THE LOTUS EATERS (2007); Nasser Hussain, THE JURISPRUDENCE OF EMERGENCY: COLONIALISM AND THE RULE OF LAW (2003); and Achilles Mbembe, ON THE POSTCOLONY (2001). *See also* Jacques Derrida, *The Mystical Foundations of Authority* in Gil Anidjar (ed.), ACTS OF RELIGION (2001).

397 *See* Stewart Chang, *The Postcolonial Problem for Gay Rights*, 32 Boston Univ. Int'l. L.J. 309–354 (2014). Another example of this type of superimposition of values is the sex tourism industry, *see e.g.*, Patrick Vrancken and Kasturi Chetty, *International Child Sex Tourism- An African Perspective*, 53(1) J. AFRICAN LAW 111–141 (April 2009).

### Feminist Legal Theories

Modern feminist legal theories can also be seen as representing stages in the movements for emancipation, equality and self-identity. Four waves can be discerned beginning in the 18th century, with proponents such as Mary Wollstonecraft. Women in this first wave advocated for their emancipation from husbands and fathers, equal treatment, voting rights and the recognition of women's basic human rights. Invoking a liberal argument, the endeavor was for equal treatment under the law in the belief that once this was achieved, women would be on parity with men.[398]

The second wave is defined by radical feminist legal theory beginning in the 1960's. Radical feminism criticized the liberal reformist approach of the first wave as dominated by white, Western middle class heterosexual women. Sexuality and reproductive rights became central issues, as seen from the writings of Catherine MacKinnon.[399] The subjugation of women was the result of the patriarchy, women's roles as wives and mothers, normative heterosexuality and capitalism. Sex and gender were differentiated, the former biological, and the latter a social construct varying from culture-to-culture and over time. Feminism was about breaking down gender stereotypes for both men and women,[400] with the understanding that the "personal is political." It was not enough to simply pass laws to insure equal treatment, the legal structures and society needed to be totally rehauled.

Third wave feminism began in the mid-1990's, influenced by post-modernism, intersectionality, and the backlash to the efforts made to date with respect to equality under both the liberal and radical efforts. The third wave argues that the essentialism of radical legal feminist theory is too narrowly focused on one view of feminism.[401] Instead, there is a need for multiple feminisms, as raised in bell hooks' seminal book, Ain't I a woman.[402] Race, gender and sexuality, and issues of individual emancipation are cornerstones in the third wave. The focus no longer is only on women, with many third-wavers rejecting the label of "feminist."

---

398 This history and summary is taken from Martha Rampton, *Four Waves of Feminism*, PACIFIC MAGAZINE (2008).

399 *See* Catharine MacKinnon, FEMINISM UNMODIFIED: DISCOURSES ON LIFE AND LAW (Harvard 1987).

400 *See also* Raewyin Connell, MASCULINITIES (1st ed. 1993, 2nd ed. Cambridge 2005).

401 *See* Elizabeth Evans, THE POLITICS OF THIRD WAVE FEMINISMS NEOLIBERALISM, INTERSECTIONALITY, AND THE STATE IN BRITAIN AND THE US (Palgrave 2015).

402 *See* bell hooks, AIN'T I A WOMAN: BLACK WOMEN AND FEMINISM (1st ed. 1981, 2nd ed. Routledge 2015).

Fourth wave feminism criticizes the third wave for its perceived complacency as to equality achievements for women.[403] The fourth wave has a renewed awareness of the problems women are still facing, much the same as those articulated in the 1960's, sexual violence, employment discrimination and objectification. These issues are now nuanced with perspectives taken up by the Third Wave, speaking in terms of intersectionality whereby:

> [W]omen's suppression can only fully be understood in a context of the marginalization of other groups and genders—feminism is part of a larger consciousness of oppression along with racism, ageism, classism, abelism, and sexual orientation (no "ism" to go with that) … Feminism no longer just refers to the struggles of women; it is a clarion call for gender equity.[404]

Each of these waves are today still vibrant in some form, and have in their turn generated a number of feminist legal theories, too many to give them the attention they deserve in this limited space.[405] A short list of feminist legal theories can include liberal, radical, essentialist (cultural), postmodern, postliberal, Marxist, socialist, critical race, global critical race, Nordic gender studies, masculinities, postcolonial, Queer theory and intersectionality.

### Queer Legal Theory

Queer legal theories[406] address the heteronormative assumptions of society, examining issues central to lesbian, gay, bisexual, transgender, queer and questioning, intersex and intergender and anonymous and ally individuals. Issues such as the repeal of anti-sodomy laws, gender reassignment without sterilization, the rights to marriage, children, adoption, fertilization procedures have been at the forefront of these efforts.

The conflation of sex, gender, and sexual orientation as social and legal constructs facilitating discrimination against individuals outside these imagined constructs was an initial focus of Queer Legal Theory, analyzing how the use

---

403 *See also* Ealasaid Munro, *Feminism, A Fourth Wave?* 4 POLITICAL INSIGHT 22–25 (2013).

404 Rampton, *Four Waves of Feminism*.

405 For an overview of feminist legal theories, *see* Margaret Davies (ed.) and Vannesso Munro, THE ASHGATE RESEARCH COMPANION TO FEMINIST LEGAL THEORY (Routledge 2013).

406 For an overview of Queer Theory, *see* Noreen Giffney and Michael O'Rourke (eds.), THE ASHGATE RESEARCH COMPANION TO QUEER THEORY (Routledge 2009).

of a sex binary construct further perpetuates systemic discrimination.[407] This approach has been expanded to a more multi-dimensional analysis, moving beyond sexual orientation to include multiple diverse sexual minorities and the intersections for example, of race, class and religion.[408] Global gay rights, issues of post-colonialism and essentialism have also been brought into these analyses.[409]

### Intersectionality and the Law

Kimberlé Crenshaw broadened CRT first to Critical Race Feminism then to a theory of Intersectionality, based partly on the sex-plus approach of the courts.[410] Intersectionality facilitates a focus on individuals whose subject-positions are formed by multiple and hybrid interests:

> [T]he interplay between individual versus structural sources of equality as well as the mutual construction of racism with other forms of 'isms,' such as class-based oppression, gender-based oppression, and other inequalities based on religion, sexual orientation, immigration status, and so on—what is sometimes called intersectionality or simultaneity.[411]

---

407 *See* Damian A. Gonzalez-Salzberg, *The Accepted Transsexual and the Absent Transgender: A Queer reading of the Regulation of Sex/Gender by the European Court of Human Rights*, 29(4) AM. UNIV. INT'L. L. REV. 797–830 (2014).

408 *See* Francisco Valdes, *Beyond Sexual Orientation in Queer Legal Theory: Majoritarianism, Multidimensionality, and Responsibility in Social Justice Scholarship or Legal Scholars as Cultural Warriors Symposium: InterSEXionality: Interdisciplinary Perspectives on Queering Legal Theory: Afterword*, 75 DENV. U. L. REV. 1409–1464, 1411 (1997–1998). *See also* Merry E. Wiesner-Hanks, *Crossing borders in transnational gender history*, 6(3) J. GLOBAL HISTORY 357–379 (2011).

409 Laurie Rose Kepros, *Queer Theory: Weed or Seed in the Garden of Legal Theory?*, 9 LAW & SEXUALITY REV. LESBIAN GAY BISEXUAL & LEGAL ISSUES 279–310 (1999–2000). *See also* Francisco Valdes, *Queers, Sissies, Dykes, and Tomboys: Deconstructing the Conflation of "Sex," "Gender," and "Sexual Orientation"*, 83(1) EURO-AM. LAW AND SOCIETY 1–377 (1995). As to the possible tensions between Feminism and Queer legal theory, *see* Martha Albertson Fineman, Jack E. Jackson, Adam P. Romero (eds.), FEMINIST AND QUEER LEGAL THEORY. INTIMATE ENCOUNTERS, UNCOMFORTABLE CONVERSATIONS (Ashgate 2009).

410 Kimberlé Crenshaw, *Demarginalizing the Intersection of Race and Sex: A Black Feminist Critique of Antidiscrimination Doctrine, Feminist Theory and Antiracist Politics*, 1(8) UNIV. CHICAGO LEGAL FORUM 139 (1989).

411 Chon 648. *See also* Crenshaw, *Mapping the Margins: Intersectionality, Identity Politics & Violence Against Women of Color*, 43 STAN. L. REV.1241–99 (1994).

Intersectionality argues that these groupings must be recognized, as certain groups are favored and disfavored, consequently perpetuating discrimination.[412] By recognizing these intersectional groups, protections against discrimination are extended to a greater number of groups suffering from this double jeopardy of discrimination.

Scholars have mobilized intersectionality to engage "multiple axes of difference—class, sexual orientation, nation, citizenship, immigration status, disability, and religion and not just race and gender. And they have employed the theory to analyze a range of complex social processes—classism, homophobia, xenophobia, nativism, ageism, ableism, and Islamophobia not just anti-Black racism and sexism."[413] A seen from the short descriptions above, these theories interweave with each other in the efforts to reveal the fundamental stereotypes and assumptions underlying much of the law.

### *Final Remarks*

The field of discrimination protections is characterized by its evolutionary nature, particularly with respect to the protected grounds chosen by the different legal structures. In modern times, the industrialization of the North Atlantic slave trade is the ultimate driving factor to international, regional and national discrimination protections, beginning with the international agreements to end the institution. The catalogue of protected grounds within the 1948 United Nations Declaration of Human Rights has created a dialogue with every

---

412 Aisha Nicole Davis, *Intersectionality and International Law: Recognizing Complex Identities on the Global Stage*, 28 HARVARD HUMAN RIGHTS J. 268 (2015). *See generally* Darren Rosenblum, *Queer Intersectionality and the Failure of Recent Lesbian and Gay "Victories"*, 4 L. & SEXUALITY REV. LESBIAN & GAY L. ISSUES 83 (1994); Lisa Bowleg, *When Black +Lesbian + Woman ≠ Black Lesbian Woman: The Methodological Challenges of Qualitative and Quantitative Intersectionality Research*, 59 SEX ROLES 312 (2008); Avtar Brah and Ann Phoenix, *Ain't I a Woman? Revisiting Intersectionality*, 5 J. INT'L WOMEN'S STUD. 75, 82 (2004); John O. Calmore, *A Call to Context: The Professional Challenges of Cause Lawyering at the Intersection of Race, Space, and Poverty*, 67 FORDHAM L. REV. 1927 (1999); David F. Warner and Tyson H. Brown, *Understanding How Race/Ethnicity and Gender Define Age-Trajectories of Disability: An Intersectionality Approach*, 72 SOC. SCI. & MED. 1236 (2011); and Linda R. Shaw, Fong Chan and Brian T. McMahon, *Intersectionality and Disability Harassment: The Interactive Effects of Disability, Race, Age, and Gender*, 55 REHABILITATION COUNSELING BULLETIN 82 (2012). For a comparative work on intersectionality, *see* Shreya Atrey, REALISING INTERSECTIONALITY IN DISCRIMINATION LAW (D.Phil. Oxford 2015).

413 Devon W. Carbado, *Colorblind Intersectionality*, 38(4) SIGNS: INTERSECTIONALITY: THEORIZING POWER, EMPOWERING THEORY 811–845, 815 (2013).

regional cooperation, and most if not all nations. The protections have been expanded in certain systems to include age, disability, genetic integrity, sexual orientation and transgender issues, while other UNDHR grounds are not as prevalent as protection discrimination grounds in other legal systems, such as language, political or other opinion, national or social origin, property, birth or other status. The historical view provided in this volume demonstrates how important the developments internationally, regionally and nationally have been for strengthening discrimination protections, with each level serving as sources of inspiration as well as markers as to the legal efforts made. The impact of EU law on both the UK and Sweden is very apparent, with legislation enacted to harmonize with the protections afforded by the directives. A second aspect that also becomes imperative in such a comparison is the need for individuals to actually be able to successfully make claims, access to justice issues that must be addressed hand-in-hand with any discrimination legislation in order for true protections to exist. This latter aspect is also heavily emphasized in the developments of the different legal theoretical approaches to issues such as sex, gender, race, sexual orientation and transgender. First waves addressed questions of equality before the law, while later theories look to issues of social constructs, substantive justice and access to justice. On a last note, this work began with the modern legal treatment of the institution of slavery beginning in the 18th century. Though that may feel distant, in 2015 the United Nations estimated that twenty-one million individuals still live in slavery.[414]

This first volume in the Brill Research Perspectives series concerning comparative discrimination law sets out the historical development of issues of discrimination protection in international, regional and certain national bases. Several of the theoretical frameworks invoked in a comparative discrimination analysis are addressed, either as institutional frameworks or theories addressing specific grounds. Justice cannot be done in such a short volume as to the efforts of literally the millions of individuals who have fought for issues of equality and recognition. The aim has been to give the reader a platform from which to undertake further reading and research in the compelling topic of comparative discrimination law.

414 United Nations Secretary-General Ban Ki-moon, *Statement for the International Day for the Abolition of Slavery*, 2 December 2015, available at the UN website, un.org: "Slavery has many modern forms, from the children toiling as domestic servants, farmhands and factory workers, to the bonded labourers struggling to pay off ever-mounting debts, to the victims of sex trafficking who endure horrific abuse."

## Appendix 1: Chronology of the Different Protected Grounds

*Table of the different explicit protected discrimination grounds*

| Ground | 1945<br>US<br>New York | 1948 UNDHR<br>1965 ICERD<br>1966 ICCPR<br>& ICESCR<br>1979 CEDAW<br>1989 CRC<br>1990 CMW<br>2006 CRPD | 1948<br>OAS | 1950<br>COE<br>ECHR<br><br>1996<br>Charter | ILO<br>Conv | 1955<br>US<br>MN |
|---|---|---|---|---|---|---|
| Race | 1945 | 1948<br>1965<br>1966<br>1989<br>1990 | 1948 | 1950<br>1961<br>1996 | 1958 | 1955 |
| Colour | 1945 | 1948<br>1965<br>1966<br>1989<br>1990 | | 1950<br>1961<br>1996 | 1958 | 1955 |
| Sex | 1968 | 1948<br>1966<br>1979<br>1989<br>1990<br>2006 | 1948<br>2013 | 1950<br>1961<br>1996 | 1951<br>1958 | 1971 |
| Women | | 1979 | | | | |
| Language | | 1948<br>1966<br>1989<br>1990 | 1967<br>2013 | 1950<br>1996<br>2013 | | |
| Religion | 2002 | 1948<br>1966<br>1989<br>1990 | 2013 | 1950<br>1961<br>1996<br>2013 | 1958 | 1955 |

| 959 s ali | EU Dir 1999 Char | 1963 US | 1965 UK | 1978 SWEDENt | 1981 African Charter | 1990 OIC | 1995 CIS | 2004 Arab Charter |
|---|---|---|---|---|---|---|---|---|
| 959 | 1999 D2000 | 1964 | 1965 | 1999 (removed) | 1981 | 1990 | 1995 | 2004 |
| 959 | 1999 | 1964 | 1965 | | 1981 | 1990 | 1995 | 2004 |
| 970 | 1999 T1957 D1975 | 1964 | 1970 EPA 1975 | 1979 | 1981 | 1990 | 1995 | 2004 |
| | D1999 | | | | 2003 1981 | 1990 | 1995 | 2004 |
| | D2000 | 1964 | 2003 | 1999 | 1981 | 1990 | 1995 | 2004 |

*Table of the different explicit protected discrimination grounds* (cont.)

| Ground | 1945 US New York | 1948 UNDHR<br>1965 ICERD<br>1966 ICCPR & ICESCR<br>1979 CEDAW<br>1989 CRC<br>1990 CMW<br>2006 CRPD | 1948 OAS | 1950 COE ECHR<br>1996 Charter | ILO Conv | 1955 US MN |
|---|---|---|---|---|---|---|
| Creed | 1945 | | 1948 | | | 1955 |
| Political or other opinion | | 1948<br>1966<br>1989<br>1990 | 2013 | 1950<br>1961<br>1996 | 1958 | |
| National origin | 1945 | 1948<br>1965<br>1966<br>1990 | | 1950<br>1961<br>1996 | 1958 | 1955 |
| Social origin | | 1948<br>1966<br>1989<br>1990 | 2013 | 1950<br>1961<br>1996 | 1958 | |
| Ancestry | | | 1948 | | | |
| Cultural Identity | | | 2013 | | | |
| Social condition | | | 1948 | | | |
| Migrant | | 1990 | 2013 | | | |
| Refugee | | | 2013 | | | |
| Repatriate | | | 2013 | | | |
| Property | | 1948<br>1966<br>1989<br>1990 | | 1950 | | |
| Birth status | | 1948<br>1966<br>1989<br>1990 | | 1950<br>1996 | | |

| 959 US Cali | EU Dir 1999 Char | 1963 US | 1965 UK | 1978 SWEDENt | 1981 African Charter | 1990 OIC | 1995 CIS | 2004 Arab Charter |
|---|---|---|---|---|---|---|---|---|
| 959 | | | | | | | | |
| | 1999 | | 2010 | | 1981 | 1990 | 1995 | 2004 |
| | 1999 | 1964 | 1965 | | 1981 | | | 2004 |
| | 1999 | | | | 1981 | | 1995 | 2004 |
| 995 | | | | | | | | |
| | | | | | | | | |
| | | | | | | 1990 | | |
| | | | | | | | | |
| | | | | | | | | |
| | | | | | | | | |
| | 1999 | | | | | | 1995 | 2004 |
| | 1999 | | | | 1981 | | 1995 | 2004 |

*Table of the different explicit protected discrimination grounds* (cont.)

| Ground | 1945<br>US<br>New York | 1948 UNDHR<br>1965 ICERD<br>1966 ICCPR<br>& ICESCR<br>1979 CEDAW<br>1989 CRC<br>1990 CMW<br>2006 CRPD | 1948<br>OAS | 1950<br>COE<br>ECHR<br><br>1996<br>Charter | ILO<br>Conv | 1955<br>US<br>MN |
|---|---|---|---|---|---|---|
| Other status | | 1948<br>1966<br>1989<br>1990 | | 1950<br>1996 | | |
| Children | | 1989<br>2006 | | | | |
| Pregnancy | 2003 | | | | | |
| Families | 1991 | | | | | |
| Descent | | 1965 | | | | |
| National Minority | | | | 1950<br>1996 | | |
| Association with a national minority | | | 1996 | | | |
| Ethnic Origin/ Group | | 1965<br>1989<br>1990 | 2001 | | | |
| Marital status | 1991 | 1979<br>1990 | | | | 1971 |
| Disability | 1984 | 2006 | 2013 | | | 1971 |
| Legal Status | | 1990 | 2013 | | | |
| Nationality | | 1990 | 1948<br>2013 | | | |
| Age | 1971 | 1990 | 2013 | | | |
| Economic position/ status | | 1990 | 2013 | | | |
| Fortune | | 1989 | | | | |
| Health | | | 2013 | 1996 | | |

| 959 's 'ali | EU Dir 1999 Char | 1963 US | 1965 UK | 1978 SWEDENt | 1981 African Charter | 1990 OIC | 1995 CIS | 2004 Arab Charter |
|---|---|---|---|---|---|---|---|---|
| | | | | | 1981 | | 1995 | |
| | | | | | | | | |
| 979 | D1992 | 1978 | 2010 | 1978 | | | | |
| | | | | | | | | |
| | 1999 | | | | | | 1995 | |
| | | | | | | | | |
| | 1999 D2000 | | 1965 | 1999 | 1981 | | | |
| ,009 | | | 2010 | | | | | |
| 973 | 1999 D2000 | 1990 | 1995 | 1999 | | | | 2004 |
| | | | | | | | | |
| | 1999 | | | | | | | |
| ,009 | 2000 | 1967 | 2006 | 2008 | | | | |
| | | | | | | | | |
| | | | | | | | | |

*Table of the different explicit protected discrimination grounds* (cont.)

| Ground | 1945 US New York | 1948 UNDHR 1965 ICERD 1966 ICCPR & ICESCR 1979 CEDAW 1989 CRC 1990 CMW 2006 CRPD | 1948 OAS | 1950 COE ECHR 1996 Charter | ILO Conv | 1955 US MN |
|---|---|---|---|---|---|---|
| Genetic Features Genetic Information | 2003 | | 2013 | | | |
| Sexual Orientation | 2003 | | 2013 | | | 1993 |
| Military Status | 1993 | | | | | |
| Family Leave Medical Condition | | | | | | |
| Public Assistance | | | | | | 1971 |
| Familial Status | 2016 | | | | | 2014 |
| Gender | 2016 | | 2001 | | | 1993 |
| Gender identity, Gender expression | 2016 | | 2013 | | | 1993 |
| Gender reassignment | | | | | | |
| Educational level | | | 2013 | | | |

| 959 s ali | EU Dir 1999 Char | 1963 US | 1965 UK | 1978 SWEDENt | 1981 African Charter | 1990 OIC | 1995 CIS | 2004 Arab Charter |
|---|---|---|---|---|---|---|---|---|
| | 1999 | | | | | | | |
| 000 | | 2008 | | | | | | |
| 992 | 1999 D2000 | | 2003 | 1999 | | | | |
| | | | | | | | | |
| 009 | | | 1996 | 1978 | | | | |
| 009 | | | | | | | | |
| | | | | | | | | |
| 992 | | | | | | | | |
| 003 | | | | | | | | |
| 003 | | | | 2008 | | | | |
| | | | 2010 | | | | | |
| | | | | | | | | |

## Reading List

Jean Allain, The Law and Slavery, Prohibiting Human Exploitation (Brill 2015).
Sandra Fredman, Discrimination Law (2nd ed. Oxford 2011).
Sandra Fredman and Meghan Campbell, Social and Economic Rights and Constitutional Law (Edward Elgar 2016).
Deborah Hellman and Sophia Moreau, The Philosophical Foundations of Discrimination Law (Oxford 2013).
Micheline R. Ishay, The History of Human Rights From Ancient Times to the Globalization Era (2nd ed. University of California Press 2008).
Tarunabh Khaitan, A Theory of Discrimination Law (Oxford 2015).
Samuel Moyn, Human Rights and the Uses of History: Expanded (2nd ed. 2017).
David B. Oppenheimer, Sheila R. Foster, Sora Y. Han, Comparative Equality and Anti-Discrimination Law (Foundation Press 2012).
Malcom Sargeant, Discrimination and the Law (Routledge 2013).
Iyiola Solanke, Discrimination as Stigma—A Theory of Anti-Discrimination Law (Hart 2017).

www.ingramcontent.com/pod-product-compliance
Lightning Source LLC
Chambersburg PA
CBHW031327230926
51848CB00001B/124